EXPLORE THE LEADERSHIP PRINCIPLES THAT MADE SARAH PALIN SUCCESSFUL

★

OUR PRESENT ERA DEMANDS A NEW STYLE OF leadership that transcends political affiliation and party lines. In an age that values relationship over authority and instant information over accuracy, breadth of knowledge and depth of conviction are prized commodities. Governor Sarah Palin (R–Alaska) brings both of those qualities to her new role as candidate for the vice presidency of the United States. Her familiarity with a broad range of issues and her strong moral center are just two of the leadership traits that have allowed Palin to organize and focus her efforts in elected office. Exploring themes from her career in politics, her life as a hockey mom, and her strongly held Christian faith, author Joseph Hilley's biographical leadership study of Sarah Palin explores the leadership principles that have catapulted her into the national spotlight and explains how she models a fresh paradigm of leadership that will guide our nation through the twenty-first century.

Novels by Joe Hilley

Sober Justice

Double Take

Electric Beach

Night Rain

The Deposition

SARAH PALIN

A New Kind of Leader

JOE · HILLEY

ZONDERVAN®

ZONDERVAN.com/
AUTHORTRACKER
follow your favorite authors

ZONDERVAN®

Sarah Palin
Copyright © 2008 by Joseph Hilley

This title is also available as a Zondervan ebook.
Visit www.zondervan.com/ebooks.

This title is also available in a Zondervan audio edition.
Visit www.zondervan.fm.

Requests for information should be addressed to:

Zondervan, *Grand Rapids, Michigan 49530*

ISBN 978-0-310-31892-7

Joseph Hilley is represented by Thomas J. Winters and Jeffrey C. Dunn of
Winters, King & Associates, Inc., Tulsa, Oklahoma.

All Scripture quotations, unless otherwise indicated, are taken from the *Holy
Bible, New International Version®*. NIV®. Copyright © 1973, 1978, 1984 by International Bible Society. Used by permission of Zondervan. All rights reserved.

Interior design by Beth Shagene

Printed in the United States of America

08 09 10 11 12 13 • 21 20 19 18 17 16 15 14 13 12 11 10 9 8 7 6 5 4 3 2 1

A good leader inspires people
to have confidence in the leader;
a great leader inspires people
to have confidence in themselves.

Anonymous

CONTENTS

HISTORY IN THE MAKING

By Chuck Colson

★

Recently, over 40 million TV viewers watched Barack Obama become the first African-American nominee of a major political party. And 24 hours later, Republican candidate John McCain set the political world on its ear by selecting a little-known woman governor from Alaska, Sarah Palin, as his running mate.

Either way the election turns out, history will be made. The 2008 Presidential Election will be a groundbreaking, ceiling-shattering event regardless of the new administration that takes office. History is in the making before our very eyes. And the clash of worldviews is nowhere more evident than in the reaction to Palin's nomination as vice president.

Social conservatives reacted to Palin's selection with near euphoria. Social liberals reacted with fury. Why? How could a governor from a politically small state spark such strong emotions? What is it about Palin that has turned her candidacy into a lightning rod for the political establishment as well as public opinion? Is it the fact that she's breaking glass ceilings as a female political leader or that she's coming to center stage from relative national obscurity?

No. It is because she does not fit the feminist stereotype. She's just a high-achieving mom who comes from the common people. Consider every major controversial issue in American politics and culture right now and somehow, they touch her personally. Start with the most obvious: abortion.

Palin, a mother of five, is staunchly pro-life. And, as you likely know by now, her fifth child, Trig, has Down syndrome. Knowing full well the challenges such a baby would become, Mrs. Palin chose to bring the baby to term. Then, shortly after her selection was announced, Palin and her husband announced that their oldest daughter was pregnant out-of-wedlock—and that the daughter would have the baby.

People on both sides of the life issue reacted swiftly. The pro-abortion crowd mocked Palin for her support of abstinence-only sex education, which, they say, failed her own daughter. Some commentators took the *ad hominem* approach, claiming that it is fine for Mrs. Palin and her daughter to bring their babies to term; after all, they've got money and a supportive family. At the same time, the pro-life side hailed Palin and her daughter as heroes for living out what they believe.

However, I believe that we ought to look at this situation as a test for ourselves. Would *your* belief in the sanctity of life have stood the test if you had found yourself in the Palins' situation? Either as a middle-aged working mom, or as the father of a pregnant teenage girl? How supportive is your church of young, unwed mothers? How do you respond to teen mothers in your neighborhood? How does your willingness to see someone else's point of view affect the social and political choices you make?

Next, consider the war in Iraq. Mrs. Palin's oldest son, Track, enlisted in the Army and has deployed to Iraq. Critics of the war have not said much about this young man's love of country. But his actions, like those of his mother, should cause those who support the war to reflect for a moment: How would you react to your son's enlisting? For putting his money where his mouth is, so to speak? Regardless of where you stand in theory, the war on terror takes on a new, personal dimension when your own flesh and blood leaves home to risk his life for our country.

With Governor Palin, the issues converge in a way that transcends rhetoric and becomes reality. She has experienced all the dilemmas we all live with in everyday life. Pick any issue ... homosexual "marriage": She is against it. But her first act as governor of Alaska was to veto legislation that would have denied state-funded health benefits for gay partners. Or oil drilling: She is for it—even in the Alaska National Wildlife Refuge, and even though she loves the great outdoors as a hunter. Earmarks? She helped scuttle the infamous Bridge to Nowhere. But it also seems that as a small-town mayor, she hired lobbyists to help secure millions in federal dollars to benefit her community.

Like all of us, she wrestles with her own convictions. Every flashpoint in American politics and culture seems to come together in this woman from Alaska. I do not believe Christian leaders should make partisan endorsements, so I am not telling you how to vote, but I am aware that Sarah Palin's leadership offers a breath of fresh air to the often stagnant political world of competing agendas and partisan loyalties. Why? Because she personally struggles with the same tensions that affect all of us and maintains her commitment to convictions.

In *Sarah Palin: A New Kind of Leader*, Joe Hilley makes the case that Palin's leadership exemplifies a new style of political leader, one grounded by her faith while riding the winds of change. If she is elected, all sides can agree: There will be change in Washington.

CHAPTER 1

FROM WASILLA TO WASHINGTON

I was just your average hockey mom,
and signed up for the PTA because I wanted
to make my kids' public education better.

Sarah Palin

History never looks like history
when you are living through it.

John W. Gardner

OUTSIDE THE NUTTER CENTER AT WRIGHT STATE University, the sky was clear and blue, the air hot and humid. Long lines of McCain supporters stretched from the entry doors down the sidewalks and across the parking lot. Two and three abreast they waited, hoping for a chance to get inside the building. Around them, vendors with pushcarts hawked their wares selling McCain t-shirts, bumper stickers, and assorted campaign items.

Inside the Nutter Center, home of the Wright State Raiders basketball team, a loud and boisterous crowd packed every available seat. They had been gathered there since the doors opened three hours earlier. Sitting shoulder to shoulder, they waited for the candidate to arrive. Restless, nervous, and pensive, their voices settled over the arena in a collective murmur.

At noon the lights went down and the arena turned

dark. The crowd gave a spontaneous gasp in response. Then loud speakers, suspended from a scoring gondola above center court, blared music at a deafening volume. In the darkness the crowd waved glow sticks they had been handed at the door when they arrived. The scene looked and sounded like a rock concert.

A few minutes later, the Republican presidential candidate appeared in the corner at one end of the arena. As the music faded, a clear, crisp voice from the speakers announced his presence, and then he made his way onto the court.

Walking with his wife and daughter, John McCain moved down a navy blue carpet laid along the end line of the basketball court. Near the spot where the goal would have hung, they paused, waved to the crowd, then made their way toward center court. There a podium stood atop a newly constructed dais. The candidate and his family stepped slowly toward it, still waving to the crowd as they went. As he reached the podium, McCain paused again and scanned the crowd. His wife and daughter, looking excited and nervous, stepped back, hands folded at the waist. This was his day, his moment. No one wanted it more for him than they did.

After a minute or two to accept the crowd's adulation, McCain stepped to the podium and opened his mouth to speak. Just then a chorus of male voices rose from his right, singing a hearty rendition of "Happy Birthday."

McCain seemed to relish the singers, even though they sounded like drunken sailors, and seemed glad they had remembered the day. As the song faded, he turned again to the podium and set his mouth to speak. Before he could begin, another chorus was heard, more faint than the first but equally well received. It was followed by a third. Finally, the crowd grew quiet. McCain stepped forward and faced them from behind the podium.

Halfway down the remainder of the court, near the foul line on the opposite end, a bank of television cameras focused on the candidate. Wired and ready, cameramen zoomed in for a tighter shot, capturing McCain and the blue-and-white campaign sign that hung from the front with a crowd of people in the stands behind him. On their feet now, they were wedged in tight against each other. Many held small American flags. Facing the back of McCain's head, they stared up at jumbo television screens on the scoring gondola high above.

Visible in the stands was a woman with short, dark hair, wearing jeans and a black scooped-neck top. A nameless face in the crowd. She could have been anyone's mother as her reactions typified millions across the nation. With her eyes trained on the television screen, she took no notice of the camera pointed in her direction as it caught her every move.

John McCain had come to the outskirts of Dayton, Ohio, to end what had been months of speculation about his selection of a vice presidential running mate. Intent on capturing for himself the title "Candidate of Change," McCain had selected the site for obvious reasons.

Located in America's heartland, Wright State was named for two of the nation's most innovative minds, Orville and Wilbur Wright. Using tenacity and stubborn resolve, the brothers had applied their imagination and ingenuity to the problem of manned flight, a cause most thought hopeless. Working in their bicycle shop just down the road, they fashioned a fragile craft of wood and paper and found a solution to a seemingly unsolvable riddle. The next winter they took their winged craft to the windswept beaches of North Carolina and soared into history, leaving behind an indelible mark on the twentieth century.

Tenacity and stubborn resolve were two things McCain knew well. They had kept him alive through the dark hours of confinement in the prison camps of North Vietnam. Long cast as a maverick, he was about to show the world the ingenuity that only his closest friends and family had appreciated. He, like the Wright brothers, was an aviator. What better place for a pilot to enjoy such a momentous occasion? The Wrights had been first in their century. He was about to be first in his. It was a hint no one in the audience seemed to catch.

McCain began his remarks slowly, thanking the crowd for their patience and acknowledging his birthday. Then, turning to the subject at hand, he seemed to savor each word. He carefully described the selection process — how he had considered and evaluated, deliberated, and debated, but in the end could choose only one. Over his shoulder, visible in the frame of the television camera, the woman in the crowd watched and listened intently.

> It's with great pride and gratitude that I tell you I have found the right partner to help me stand up to those who value their privileges over their responsibilities, who put power over principle, and put their interests before your needs.[1]

McCain, mindful of the pace, worked his delivery flawlessly, baiting the crowd with each line.

> I found someone with an outstanding reputation for standing up to special interests and entrenched bureaucracies; someone who has fought against corruption and the failed policies of the past; someone who's stopped government from wasting taxpayer's money....

A few feet away, the woman in the stands behind McCain continued to watch. Above her dark and glistening eyes, tiny wrinkles creased her forehead as she listened, anticipating the next line, trying to figure out whom he was describing.

McCain moved on through his speech and finally came around to describing the qualities of his nominee as he ticked off a list of credentials: "... knows what it's like to worry about mortgage payments and health care and the cost of gasoline and groceries."

Behind him, the woman in the stands glanced down as the frown on her forehead gave way to a cloud of uncertainty across her face. Her eyes darted anxiously from side to side.

Still, McCain continued, "A standout high school point guard; a concerned citizen who became a member of the PTA, then a city council member, and then a mayor, and now a governor."[2]

In the stands the woman in the black shirt had a look of profound concentration. A new question now occupied her mind. She had been a member of the PTA. She worried about the mortgage and the gas and the groceries. The person McCain was describing sounded a lot like her.

"And that's why," McCain continued, his voice all but breaking with anticipation, "I am especially proud to say in the week we celebrate the anniversary of women's suffrage, a devoted ..."

Instantly, the woman's mouth fell open in a look of sudden realization. On her face was a message as plain as any written in print, visible for all who watched by television in the homes and cafes and shops across the land. She was a woman who had spent long hours toiling at home, rearing her children, driving them to baseball games and pep rallies, always behind the scenes, always wondering if anyone noticed. Now someone like her was about to take the national stage.

By then everyone in the arena knew what was going to happen. McCain the maverick was about to announce a woman as his choice for vice president.

At the podium near center court, McCain took delight in the moment, pausing long enough in his speech for just the right effect, then completing the line with a smile, "... a devoted wife and a mother of five."

The crowd roared again. McCain glanced around, his eyes sparkling in the glaring light. "I am very pleased and very privileged to introduce to you the next Vice President of the United States ... Governor Sarah Palin of the great state of Alaska."

Around him the crowd sounded their approval with thunderous applause and stomping feet. Raising her hands high above her head, the woman in the stands behind him began to dance,[3] and with her, the nation came alive.

✭

Within minutes of John McCain's announcement, newscasters and pundits across the nation swung into action. In their droll and erudite way, they digested the scant information revealed about Palin in the remarks made before the Dayton crowd. By the end of the first hour, their commentary had exhausted the sparse details of her life and had moved on to a discussion of the implications in the event the nation and the world had just witnessed. As reporters talked, news of the announcement swept the countryside, and before the second hour had passed, everyone from Maine to California was enveloped in the story. Awakened and roused like never before, they jammed websites and blogs to search for information about the new vice presidential candidate, the woman from Wasilla.

In Juneau, the State of Alaska's official website received so many hits it crashed as technicians struggled to keep it online. In tiny Wasilla, the mayor's office where Palin once had served was swamped with requests for news about her life and family. Before the day was over, the streets would be filled with satellite trucks, rental cars, and people on foot, each one clamoring for details of her life.

Newscasters were right to note that Sarah Palin's nomination had changed the election's landscape. Since she was the first woman to occupy a Republican ticket for national office, her selection marked a shift in the party's center. Commentators were quick to point out she had been Wasilla's first female mayor and the first woman elected governor of Alaska, but they were wrong to think the change they had noticed applied only to the current campaign.

Doubtless, the 2008 presidential election will be known as one of the most startling examples of electoral politics yet witnessed in our country's history. While one major party nominated the first African American for the nation's highest office, its rival party selected its first female for the nation's vice president. Regardless of the outcome, this moment in political history marks a time of unprecedented change, as barriers of gender and race once thought impenetrable shatter into millions of pieces.

Both presidential candidates, Barack Obama and John McCain, touted political reform and fresh perspectives in a heated contest of positions and ideas as diverse as the nation itself. Faced with the seemingly intractable issues of a slowing economy, war in Iraq, and expanding reliance on foreign oil, the American people were weary of partisan politics and bickering. The time had come to invigorate the campaign process — a process jaded with cynicism and gridlocked hope.

For Democrat contender Obama, a United States senator from Illinois, a new approach meant reliance on eloquence and unbridled enthusiasm for innovation. Fresh and untainted by politics as usual, his inexperience made him seem new and extraordinarily alive. Yet that inexperience — the very thing that made him fresh—left him vulnerable to attack as young and untried, having just arrived in the Senate from the Illinois legislature. To balance the ticket, Obama turned to a familiar party leader and career politician, Senator Joseph Biden, as his running mate.

Across the aisle, John McCain, the Republican nominee and senator from Arizona, found himself in a precarious position. With approval ratings for the current Republican administration hovering at historic lows, McCain was forced to distance himself from the incumbent, President George W. Bush. To do that, McCain emphasized his role as a political maverick rather than party stalwart, a distinction not altogether untrue. Yet his experience—the thing that gave him cache with moderate voters—left him appearing old, outdated, and bound in the strictures of traditional politics. In need of adding balance, he selected as his running mate a governor—one who was female, young, and relatively unknown to the national political spotlight.

Sarah Palin's meteoric rise to political stardom seemed to have developed overnight. In reality, her ascent had been in the making for all of her forty-four years. In the pages that follow, you will find a survey of her life and career revealed in ten principles of leadership —qualities taken from the story of her life that offer a glimpse of who she is and how she thinks. These are the traits that have not only stood the 2008 election on its head, but have provided a model for the innovative style required of politicians by the current demands of American culture.

Many of these leadership principles will seem counterintuitive, running against the traditional formula for political success: that your weakness can be your greatest strength; sacrificing your personal ambition can unlock the path to your destiny; and removing boundaries between your public and private life can insulate you from personal attack.

In her political life, Sarah Palin has displayed many of the traits that will define successful political leaders of this century. Although far from perfect, she harbors a deep Christian faith and dogged determination to make government work for the people, rather than people for the government. Palin's style of leadership invites each of us, whatever our political bent, to embrace challenge as opportunity and difficulty as hope, characteristics that have taken her from Wasilla to the doorstep of Washington and into the heart of the nation.

CHAPTER 2

WEAKNESS IS THE NEW STRENGTH

Politics isn't just a game of clashing parties and competing interests. The right reason is to challenge the status quo, to serve the common good, and to leave this nation better than we found it.

Sarah Palin

My attitude is that if you push me
towards something that you think is a weakness,
then I will turn that perceived weakness
into a strength.

Michael Jordan

In 2002, Sarah Palin completed her last term as mayor of Wasilla, Alaska, a town located north of Anchorage with a population of some 7,500 residents. As her term drew to a close, Sarah contemplated her future. By then she had seen enough to know that Alaska faced serious challenges. She wanted to help meet those challenges and help guide the state forward, but the state was huge, the issues intertwined, the solutions complicated. Her experience seemed small, and many in the state felt a woman's place is at home. Voices from every corner told her to sit down, shut up, and let others handle it. Still, the desire in her heart to protect the state she loved, to help the people she had known all her life, and to guard the pristine wilderness that surrounded her would not go away.

Unlike some who tried to hold her back, Sarah had

actually been to the North Slope oil fields. She had hiked the coastal plains and towering mountains on foot and had plied the bays and sounds in a fishing boat. She had looked into the faces of her neighbors and seen their resolve to carve a life out of a land that, though beautiful beyond description, was often harsh and unforgiving. And every time she felt like giving up she saw those faces looking back at her. They had never given up on her; she couldn't give up on them.

In the midst of weighing her options, Sarah was approached by Frank Murkowski, Alaska's six-term United States senator, about running as lieutenant governor in the upcoming election.[1] Murkowski was returning from the United States Senate determined to become Alaska's next governor. A number of experienced Republican politicians had considered running for governor as well, but when Murkowski announced his candidacy, they all withdrew for other races. Murkowski was expected to win and win big. If Sarah could win the nomination for lieutenant governor, she would campaign alongside an Alaskan legend.[2]

The move seemed like a good one for Sarah who, in spite of her detractors, had been growing in regional prestige and political stature. Under Murkowski's tutelage, she would have an opportunity to learn from someone who had spent a lifetime in politics at both the state and national levels.

With filing day for the next election cycle approaching, Sarah mustered her courage and made a decision. She pushed aside the voices that told her she couldn't succeed, ignored those who chided her experience, and signed her name to a document declaring herself a candidate for lieutenant governor in the upcoming Republican primary. She was thirty-nine years old. By the time Primary Election Day arrived, two other Republicans had joined the race as serious contenders.[3] Sarah Palin, a mother of four from a small town far from the public eye, was in the midst of a rough-and-tumble political fight.

When the dust settled on primary night, Murkowski won the Republican governor's slot as expected. Sarah, however, came up short, finishing second to Loren Leman. Leman would go on to win the lieutenant governor's race in the general election.

That fall, Sarah campaigned tirelessly for the Republican ticket. Though disappointed at her own loss in the primary, she did her best to prove herself a team player. After all, she was young, and this was only her first attempt at statewide office. There would be more opportunities in the future, especially if the Republicans won the general election.

In November 2002 the people of Alaska elected Murkowski as governor. Most who had been watching the campaign anticipated that Sarah would receive a key appointment in the new administration. She was offered several jobs, including Commissioner of Commerce and Director of the State Parks Division. The commerce post would have been well-suited for anyone seeking elected office, but Sarah had other things on her mind. Flush with the success of her campaign, she now had her eyes open to wider possibilities. In a bold move she turned down those offers and submitted her name to fill Murkowski's vacant senate seat.

Sarah seemed like a perfect fit for Washington. She was young, energetic, and on her way up. Although outspent by her rivals in the campaign for lieutenant governor, she had finished second in the primary to the eventual winner—a remarkable showing for someone just entering the statewide political fray. Whatever the future might hold for the Alaskan Republican Party, Sarah's effort in the campaign and the public's response to her candidacy indicated she would be a part of that future. If anyone had earned a chance at the senate seat, she felt she had.

Anticipating a quick decision, Sarah watched as the new administration transitioned into office and hoped for the best. She didn't have to wait long. In what would be a sign of things to come, Murkowski announced that he had chosen his own daughter for the senate post.

Sarah ultimately accepted an appointment to the Alaska Oil and Gas Conservation Commission, a powerful agency tasked with oversight of the state's oil and gas interests. Important to the state's economy, it was nevertheless an agency that operated away from the public eye. The position afforded Sarah no real opportunity to build statewide recognition.

Even though this was not the post for which she had hoped, it put Sarah in the midst of serious decisions regarding Alaska's most vital economic resource. She dove into the task and set about learning the oil and gas business. Joining her on the commission was Randy Ruedrich, another Murkowski appointee, who was also chairman of the Alaska Republican Party.[4]

Not long after her appointment, Sarah was named chairman of the commission. That title brought with it the additional responsibility of serving as the commission's ethics officer. As such, she was required to file regular reports indicating any unethical activity that had been brought to her attention. Her appointment to the commission, which had seemed like a brief and minor political detour, soon became a nightmare.

As Sarah's work began on the commission, complaints emerged over what seemed like an obvious conflict of interest between Ruedrich's work as a commissioner, providing oversight to the oil and gas industry, and his position as party chairman, leading the effort to raise party funds. The oil and gas industry, as a group, formed one of the Republican Party's largest donors. Seven months after his appointment, staff complaints about Ruedrich continued to mount, with allegations that he was conducting party business on state time, leaking important documents, and favoring certain companies in the discharge of his official duties.

Sarah confronted Ruedrich with the allegations, but when the conduct continued, she contacted Murkowski's chief of staff, Jim Clark. Days went by, and nothing happened. With calls and e-mails from legislators and other officials mounting, Sarah forwarded the complaints to Gregg Renkes, the attorney general. Shortly thereafter, Ruedrich resigned.

(To this day, Ruedrich denies many of those allegations and remains chairman of the Alaska Republican Party.[5] However, in June 2004, Ruedrich reached a settlement on the ethics claims and admitted that some of the violations were true. As part of that settlement he agreed to pay a civil fine of $12,000.[6])

With Ruedrich gone, Sarah expected an ethics investigation and prompt action by the Murkowski administration. Instead, she was told to collect whatever information she found that indicated the allegations might be true and forward that evidence to the attorney general's office. After months of digging through computer files and other records, Sarah still was not assured there actually was an official investigation, but she was convinced the allegations were true.

By then, the media had picked up the story. Articles appeared raising questions and quoting conflicting sources. Consigned to silence by state law that governed the ethics allegation process, Sarah was attacked from both sides. Republicans accused her of selling out the party chairman to the Democrats, while the Democrats accused her of covering up evidence that would prove the charges true. In addition, she was becoming increasingly uncomfortable with the ethics reporting procedure. As chairman, she had to sign off on the regular ethics reports for the commission—a duty she no longer felt comfortable fulfilling.

Eleven months into the job, and with no action from the attorney general on the allegations, Sarah was in an awkward position. She could remain on the commission under the appearance of indifference to possible conflict of interest, or she could resign. For her there was no choice. She resigned and went home to Wasilla.

In all that has been written about Sarah, friends and colleagues have sometimes described the period after she resigned from the commission as a dark time for her. But that is not how she describes it. Sarah told one biographer, "It wasn't a dark time, but there was confusion. Was there something else I was supposed to [be] doing? I spent a lot of time in prayer about that."[7] In a life marked by a competitive drive to win at whatever task she tries, this statement reveals another side—one that is not intimidated by the recognition of her own human frailty.

In the silence and seclusion of those tense days, the big round sun hanging behind the mountains near her home could have looked like the sunset on her once-promising career. But thankfully for her, the mountains near her home in Wasilla lie to the east.

For many, the commission displacement would have been the end of a political career, but not for Sarah Palin. Determined and resourceful, she looked for ways to stay in the public eye and watched carefully as events unfolded. This wasn't the first time she had had to rely on instinct.

✶

BORN IN 1964 TO CHUCK AND SALLY HEATH, A HIGH SCHOOL science teacher and school secretary, Sarah Louise Palin early on found life an adventure. When she was born, the family lived in Sandpoint, Idaho. Located in Bonner County, Sandpoint sits in the upper part of the long neck of the state, just a little ways below the Canadian border. Once visited by a young Theodore Roosevelt, Sandpoint was known early in its history as a center of the region's timber industry and attendant railroads necessary to get the timber to market. Later, in the 1950s, sports-men discovered Lake Pend Oreille, and the area became popular with anglers.

When Sarah was two months old, Chuck and Sally decided to leave Idaho. By then, most of the Alaska Highway, first cut through the wilderness during World War II as a supply line for the Army, had been paved. The nation's last remaining untamed wilderness awaited those daring enough to give it a try. Chuck and Sally loaded their young and expanding family into the car and headed north to Alaska, settling first in Skagway, near the north end of the Alexander Archipelago, where Chuck taught school. Later they moved to Eagle River, an Anchorage suburb, and then to nearby Wasilla. There Sarah and her family found the town they would call home.

Nestled between the Matanuska and Susitna Valleys, the town of Wasilla lies near Anchorage at the northernmost end of Cook Inlet. Populated at first by people of hardy stock, in the nineteenth century it became a working town established as a supply point for fur trappers and gold miners come to Alaska to seek their fortune. By the time Sarah arrived, the town still retained many of those rustic qualities but was fast becoming a bedroom community for the growing city of Anchorage. The Heaths settled into a modest home and soon found their place in the rhythm of town life. Chuck took a job teaching science. Sally found work as the school secretary.

Boys in her class remember Sarah as one of the

prettiest girls in school. They also recall that she was studious and always friendly, though not flirtatious.[8] An avid sports enthusiast, she shot her first rabbit by the age of ten and, as a teenager, often rose early to hunt with her father before continuing on to school.

Two things happened to Sarah in high school that would mark her for life. She met Todd Palin, the man whom she would later marry, and she played basketball. Playing on the high school women's championship basketball team would be an experience she later described as life-changing.

After graduating from Wasilla High School in 1982, Sarah and a friend spent most of the next year in Hawaii, where they attended college. Two semesters later, Sarah grew lonesome for family, friends, and the cold climate she had grown to know and love. She returned to Wasilla, rekindled her romance with Todd Palin, and attended classes at a local community college.

In 1984, Sarah entered the Miss Wasilla beauty pageant. Viewed by her family as a frivolous endeavor, her entry in the contest caught most who knew her by surprise — so much so that it prompted a question from her brother, Chuck, about the matter. Her response was quick and incisive: "It's going to help pay my way through college."[9]

Sarah won the title of Miss Wasilla and went on to compete in the 1984 Miss Alaska pageant, placing first runner-up to the winner and receiving the Miss Congeniality award. Though uncomfortable parading before judges in a swimsuit,[10] she was thankful for the scholarship she received. With it, she attended the University of Idaho, a school located in the city of Moscow, which was south of Sandpoint and along the state's border with Washington. There she completed her undergraduate studies and earned a degree in journalism with a minor in political science.

After graduation she returned to Alaska and took a job as a television sports reporter in Anchorage. Not long after that, she and Todd Palin eloped. The young couple settled in Wasilla and began rearing a family. As her eldest son, Track, reached school age, Sarah volunteered and involved herself in trying to make the school in Wasilla a better place for her children.

For Sarah Palin, motherhood and the nurturing it entailed not only refined her character, but awakened something in her — a desire to serve, and an interest in making a difference in the life of the town where she lived. As that servant's heart grew, her thoughts turned to political office. Although she lacked specific government experience, she began to consider seeking elected office.

Sarah's lack of experience may have been a detriment to her in times gone by, when depth of knowledge and refined skill was valued in the workplace. In the past, those who sought to succeed in life were encouraged to plumb the depths of a limited area of expertise and devote their working lives to a singular effort in that one field. Things are not the same now. Today, someone with a degree in finance might work in advertising. Someone with an engineering degree might operate an online business. Next year they might switch jobs.

Part of the reason for this change is that life now offers many opportunities. Not merely more options, but opportunities. Skills are far more transferable, and more than that, the nature of how our economy produces goods and services has changed. Growing at an exponential rate, technology has empowered individuals to do for themselves what was once impossible, impractical, or cost-prohibitive. Information and empowerment are less than a computer's mouse click away. Today, more than ever, no one can know everything. No one has to. They simply need to know where to find it.

☆

SARAH HAD SERVED TWO TERMS AS MAYOR AND MADE AN unsuccessful try for lieutenant governor.[11] No one raised much of an objection to her initial foray into statewide politics. A woman in that position was no real threat to anyone. Most would have given her a deferential reaction. "Sure. She did fine as mayor. Let her have a shot. Good experience for her." But when, in 2006, she stepped up to run for the Republican nomination for governor, Sarah ran into a storm of opposition.

By then, she was no longer the darling of the party. In 2004 she had made the allegations against Ruedrich, the party chairman, that forced his resignation from the Alaska Oil and Gas Conservation Commission. In an even bolder move, the next year she had joined a Democratic state representative in filing an ethics complaint against the attorney general. (More about that later.) Ostracized by party leadership, she was forced to battle the campaign for governor on her own.

In the 2006 gubernatorial primary, the Republican establishment made the same accusations against Sarah that she had heard when she ran for mayor: No experience, and the experience she had attained was insignificant. Campaigning against Murkowski, Sarah stuck to her message, telling voters that she would listen to their concerns and that she would make government work for them. In a race that came to include five candidates, Sarah attracted more than 50 percent of the vote. In doing so, she handed the incumbent a resounding defeat and won the right to face the Democrat challenger in the general election.

In the fall campaign Sarah again heard those accusations that had become all too familiar, how she had no executive experience, didn't understand the issues, and was ill equipped for the tasks of the state's highest office. Her opponents, a former two-term Democratic governor named Tony Knowles and an Independent businessman named Andrew Halcro, did their best to portray her as uninformed and incapable.[12] Their campaign ads implied that she lacked the expertise to negotiate pipeline contracts with big oil companies and was unsuited to maintain a watchful eye on the state's rich natural resources. In a state known for its rugged terrain and difficult life, the unstated message reinforced the "old boy" network that had controlled Alaska politics for decades.

After John McCain announced her as his running mate, questions were raised once again about Sarah Palin's depth of experience. Some of the people making that charge are similar to those she faced in Alaska, men and women who have spent years in public office following in lockstep with the needs of special interest groups. If experience were a necessity, no one would ever move up.

In fact, Sarah had been gathering that experience all her life. As a mother she learned to multitask by caring for children, managing a household, and volunteering in her children's school.[13] On the PTA and city council she learned to organize, delegate, and assign tasks. She also learned the names and faces of all the people in town she didn't already know and learned to connect with them in dynamic ways.

In the office of mayor, Sarah learned about municipal funding, government contract requirements, highway construction, rail construction, and public works in a full-time job that required her to make countless decisions each day. Not contemplative, musing, ponderous decisions, but the kind that come in a constant stream. With few staff members between her and department heads, she was the one who made many of those decisions. In the course of doing that, she learned something about each of the departments. She wasn't an expert firefighter or a seasoned law enforcement officer or a public works engineer, but she didn't need to be. What she brought to the task was the ability to distill information and make decisions. That was something she had already been doing while rearing her children and managing her household. Not everyone agreed with her decisions, but she made them and moved on. In an information age, the ability to distill an issue into its working parts makes the information much easier to handle.

In America, government authority arises from six basic purposes first expressed in the Preamble to the Constitution of the United States. Those concepts include the desire to "form a more perfect union, establish justice, ensure domestic tranquility, provide for the common defense, promote the general welfare, and secure the blessings of liberty."[14] From those limited purposes, all issues can be analyzed by four succinct criteria—safety, benefit, cost, and legality. Is it safe? Will it produce a benefit? How does the cost compare to the benefit? Is the proposed action legally authorized?

As basic constitutional law issues, these four questions form the framework around which government operates and upon which good governmental decisions are made in the United States. They devolve upon the states and are expressed through their respective constitutions, notions reflected in Article One of the Alaska Constitution. Simple and direct, those four questions provide a clear and distinct means by which to parse the issues facing elected officials.

Incisive and forthright in nature, Sarah understood those concepts by instinct and used them to cut through the clutter of complex problems and reach the bottom line. Doing so, she was able to avoid becoming mired in irrelevant details. By the time she completed her service as mayor of Wasilla, Sarah Palin had mastered the art of making decisions in the information age.[15]

CHAPTER 3

SACRIFICE AMBITION TO GET AHEAD

Proverbs tell[s] us there is no strength without
unity. So ... let us be united to be strong. Let us serve
selflessly, and disregard who gets the credit.

Sarah Palin

Ambition must be made
to counteract ambition.

James Madison

WHEN SARAH PALIN WALKED INTO HER FIRST MEETING of the Parent Teachers Association, she had no idea where life would take her. One can only imagine how she must have felt. Back at home, a hundred things clamored for her attention. Her husband, a descendent of native Yupik Alaskans, had a good job in Alaska's North Slope oil field, but it took him away for long stretches.[1] Whatever had to be done at home, she was the one who had to do it. Volunteering for the PTA put one more thing on her plate, but she was willing to help and was not afraid of work. She was determined that her children would have the best classroom experience she and the school could offer.

Being the child of parents who loved sports, particularly long-distance running, Sarah learned from an early age the joy of physical exercise and a spirit of competitiveness born from a life of athletics. Her father is still an avid hunter and sports fisherman.[2] Sarah's parents gave her many things—nurturing love, a lifestyle of hard work, a warm and caring family. Her mother took her to church and was active in the congregation. Both parents were active in the schools where they worked and had a lasting effect on the lives of the students and faculty. But neither of them cared for politics or political involvement.[3]

As a member of the local PTA, Sarah was introduced to the scrappy world of civic affairs. Through this involvement she saw that the town needed improvement. Nor was she the only one who saw the need. In the words of Chas St. George, "We needed a police department. So we set up a group to make it happen."[4] That group included Sarah Palin, Mayor John Stein, Chas St. George, and Sarah's in-laws, Jim and Faye Palin.[5]

The town of Wasilla was small but growing. That growth, though welcome by most of the people who lived there, put a strain on the existing infrastructure. To address those needs, the city council passed a two percent sales tax. Businessmen derided it as the death of the town's economy. Several councilmen who were interested in developing the town's potential recruited Sarah to help beat back the anti-tax proponents.[6]

★

WHEN SARAH WOULD WORK OUT AT THE LOCAL GYM, SHE would sometimes have conversations with Mayor Stein and Irl Stambaugh, the town's new chief of police.[7] As Sarah looked for additional ways to become involved in the community, Stein and Stambaugh encouraged her to run for a seat on the city council. With the encouragement of friends and family, the idea began to grow.

Those who knew Sarah best might have been surprised that she was interested in politics, but they weren't the least concerned with whether she had the ability to campaign, win, and discharge the duties of elected office. With their support, she decided to give it a try and filed the papers to enter the 1992 election for a place on the council.

In her campaign Sarah presented herself as a "fresh face with new ideas."[8] An honest, straightforward, no-frills slogan. That's exactly what she was—a fresh face. And she brought new ideas. Everyone understood she was a mother and volunteer stepping up to the plate of community involvement, putting her time and energy behind the statements she had made about how things in town could be better. No one made much of a fuss. You can imagine morning conversation at the Kaladi Brothers Coffee shop as they gathered there before heading out in the crisp fall air. "Let her have a shot. What can it hurt? The town needs some new ideas."

After all, they had known her most of her life. She was the girl next door.

After her election to the city council and with revenue being generated by the sales tax, Sarah led the effort to build the town's infrastructure as a way of attracting more businesses. With the infrastructure in place, the local economy thrived and drove the town to a period of unprecedented growth.[9] With good fire and police protection, adequate water and sewer service and improved streets, businesses wanted to locate in the town. People living in Anchorage began to see it as a desirable place to live. Before long, "big box" retailers wanted to locate there as well. With retail options improving, people in town no longer had to drive to Anchorage in the dead of winter to buy groceries; they could shop right down the street from their house and be back in less than half the time.

Life in Wasilla was changing. Sarah Palin participated in that change and helped make it happen. Despite being young and politically untried, Sarah won that first election.[10] She wouldn't have been there if she hadn't taken that first step.[11]

Pleased by her experience on the council, she stood for re-election to a second term in 1995. Her opponents tried to raise the question of experience, but by then she had served three years. Sarah won a second term with 68 percent of the vote.[12] Using hard work and determination, and by maintaining her focus on serving the people who elected her to office, Sarah overcame those who said experience mattered most and showed them what one person with a willingness to serve can do.

☆

AFTER TWO TERMS ON THE COUNCIL, SARAH CAME TO FEEL that significant change for the city required new leadership at the top. So in 1996 she tossed her hat into the ring for election to the office of mayor at age thirty-two.

In the coffee shops and cafes around town, people sat up a little straighter. Those at city hall who had run the town for years cleared their throats and scooted up closer to their desks. You can hear their voices even now: "I ... I'm not sure she's ready. This isn't like the PTA or even city council. There's a lot of detail to this job. She's mighty young."

Sarah campaigned hard, going door-to-door to tell all who would listen about her ideas for ways to make the town better. Campaigning against an incumbent and relegated to the position of underdog, she accepted that role and used it to play up who she really was — a PTA mom, a hockey mom, trying to make life better for everyone. She could have been anyone's mother, and she didn't try to hide it. Instead, she made it work in her favor, often delivering her message while pulling her young children behind her in a red wagon.[13]

To the amazement of the town's entrenched officials, the people of Wasilla responded to Sarah's message. On election day, with the town behind her, Sarah defeated the three-term incumbent, John Stein, with a resounding 60 percent of the vote.[14]

☆

WHEN SHE BEGAN HER FIRST CAMPAIGN FOR PUBLIC office, Sarah had no idea where her efforts would lead. All she wanted was a seat on the city council. That was as far as she could see. She didn't have a roadmap showing where life would take her from there, but she wasn't afraid to embark on the journey, either.

In 2002, Sarah received something every young politician desires — the attention of those who hold higher public office. That year, as she neared her final year as mayor, the statewide election cycle came around once more. Though she entered politics with no plan for going further than the town council, by then she could see the opportunity afforded by a bigger platform, one from which she could address not only issues that affected her region but those that confronted her state. About that same time, Frank Murkowski suggested that she make a bid for lieutenant governor.

Murkowski came to politics from a career in banking. In 1970 he made an unsuccessful bid for Alaska's at-large congressional seat before winning a seat in the United States Senate in 1980. His ties ran deep in the Republican Party and in the Alaska business community.[15] Those were the ties Palin needed in order to reach a statewide office.

By 2002 the area around Wasilla had begun to shift from Democrat to Republican as more conservative voters moved out of Anchorage and into the Mat-Su Valley. A number of new Republican candidates had won election to the Alaska legislature. As Sarah approached the end of her second term as mayor, she was an obvious candidate for statewide office. What had begun as a mother's desire to contribute to a better place in which to rear her children had grown a little larger.[16]

With the help of area Republican leaders and with the backing of a concerted effort from the national party aimed at attracting younger candidates, Sarah entered the Republican primary as a candidate for lieutenant governor. Two other candidates joined in the race, but Sarah was considered by many to be the party's favorite. Although once again outspent and battling candidates with much greater name recognition than her own, she stuck to the image that had served her well, an image that was true to her personality and character. While attending a candidate's forum in Fairbanks, a moderator asked her how she would handle commissioners who failed to effectively prioritize state budgeting demands. Without hesitating, Sarah replied, "I would encourage firing the guys who can't prioritize." The crowd responded with applause.[17]

Even though she finished that race in second place, Sarah Palin looked like a fresh face on Alaska's political scene.[18] Encouraged by the outcome, she saw her defeat as an opportunity to prove she is a team player, and as an opportunity for exposure to voters while working alongside Frank Murkowski. Instead of bowing out and disappearing, she campaigned in the general election on behalf of the Republican ticket.

When Murkowski won the governor's office, the relationship created by Sarah's campaign effort paved the way for an appointment to an office in the new administration. What she wanted was his seat in the state senate. When that wasn't forthcoming, she settled for the seat on the Alaska Oil and Gas Conservation Commission.

The ensuing confrontation with fellow commissioner Randy Ruedich regarding ethical allegations left Sarah at odds with both political parties. The Republicans were unhappy because she wanted action, the Democrats because she couldn't get the action they wanted. Sarah Palin had to find new relationships or watch her political aspirations vanish.

Using her familiarity with the media that arose from her years as mayor, Sarah began to cultivate strategic relationships with reporters. Without violating secrecy laws that controlled the ethics complaint process, she placed her position on the issues raised by the Ruedrich case before reporters covering the story. When Ruedrich finally agreed to settle the charges by paying a civil fine, more of the story finally came out. Sarah was cast as the hero. Although shunned by the party regulars, she had an even stronger relationship with voters — the people who mattered most — and a growing reputation as an advocate for ethics.[19]

What looked like the end was only the beginning — a beginning that opened the door to Alaska's highest office and eventually, nomination as a candidate for vice president of the United States. Both were positions Sarah Palin could not have dreamed about when she walked into her child's school for that first PTA meeting. She attained those offices one step at a time and by following her convictions and instincts each step of the way. There was no roadmap laid out from the beginning directing her to the end. She hadn't started out with the intention of becoming governor or the Republican vice presidential nominee. She was just a mom with some ideas, looking for a place from which those ideas could be put to use.

CHAPTER 4

TRUE NORTH
NEVER CHANGES

★

… the wisdom that comes even to the captives,
by the grace of God … the special confidence of those
who have seen evil, and seen how evil is overcome.

Sarah Palin

You've got to stand for something,
or you'll fall for anything.

Aaron Tippin

AMERICA IS A RELIGIOUS COUNTRY, NEVER MORE SO THAN at election time. Unlike many presidential candidates in recent memory, Sarah Palin chose not to trot out her deep Christian commitment during her speech in Dayton, Ohio. Instead, she kept that commitment to herself and decided not to speak of her religious faith. This decision was not a new position adopted for a national campaign. Even as governor she had refused to use her position to further an overtly religious agenda.[1] Perhaps the reason for this lies in the possibility that her faith in God is so deeply rooted and intertwined in her character, a faith so integrated in her sense of self, that it defies definition apart from describing her in her entirety. The manner in which she conducts herself may not always be consistent with her convictions, yet her faith and her worldview nevertheless appear one and the same.

As a child Sarah attended the Wasilla Assembly of God with her mother and siblings. There she met the founding pastor of that church, a man named Paul Riley. With Reverend Riley and his wife as mentors, and under the watchful eye of her mother, Sarah slowly and carefully explored what it meant to be a Christian.[2] She attended Sunday morning services and participated in the youth group. As questions arose, she turned to Reverend Riley for answers. During the summer she turned twelve she was baptized by him at Little Beaver Lake Camp.[3] Her mother and siblings were baptized at the same time.[4]

The Assemblies of God falls into a strain of Christianity historically designated as Pentecostal. As a denomination the Assemblies of God traces its history to a revival that began at an Apostolic Faith Mission on Azusa Street in Los Angeles, California. Led by the Reverend William J. Seymour, an African-American minister who preached a message of racial reconciliation and who believed the biblical gifts of the Holy Spirit are still available to believers, the revival occurred in the summer of 1906. At the same time, similar revivals began to occur at other locations, primarily in the west and south. In 1914, representatives from those congregations met in Hot Springs, Arkansas, and formed the denomination. At that meeting they agreed to a statement of faith that included a full embrace of the Trinitarian concept of God.[5]

The term "Pentecostal" derives from the Jewish feast of Pentecost and from the experiences the original followers of Jesus had during that festival forty days after Jesus had been resurrected. The events of that day are recorded in the second chapter of the book of Acts in the New Testament.

Although the events of that Pentecost festival happened long ago, the Assemblies of God as a denomination believes individuals can experience a similar manifestation of the Holy Spirit today.[6] While many Christian denominations believe a person can experience the powerful, active presence of the Holy Spirit in daily life, the Assemblies of God is distinct in its belief that the Spirit gives believers the gift of a language they had not previously known, commonly referred to as the gift of tongues. Whether Sarah Palin believes all that the denomination espouses, no one knows, but this was the church environment in which she grew up.

By the time she reached her senior year, her commitment to Christ was settled. Because of this commitment and because she was an avid basketball player, she became involved in the Fellowship of Christian Athletes. As an active member and leader of FCA, it fell to her to lead the team in prayer before each game.[7] No doubt she faced the same questioning tendencies most teens confront, but through it all, her commitment to Christ was never in doubt.

As Sarah grew and became an adult with a family of her own, she and her husband brought their children to church, first to the Wasilla Assembly of God and later to Wasilla Bible Church, an independent, nondenominational congregation. Of the three churches in and around Wasilla that Sarah and her family have attended regularly, Wasilla Bible Church offers the most conservative worship style.[8] Adele Morgan, a minister of music at the church, explains, "A lot of churches are about music and media and having a big profile. We are against that. That is why it is so attractive to politicians, because they can just sit there and be safe."[9] While some critics have commented that Sarah moved to Wasilla Bible Church because of its conservative, "safer" environment, she has declined to explain such a personal choice.

⭐

IN THE TWENTY-FIRST CENTURY, ONE OF THE GREATEST challenges leaders face is that of the growing volume of information available and the pace at which that volume will increase. For each issue that arises, the government apparatus already generates thousands and thousands of pages of information.

Leaders who attempt to master the details of complex issues will find themselves buried in an avalanche of data. Swamped and even paralyzed, they will languish in the marshland of competing information and contextual complexity. To avoid this quagmire, leaders will need a strong moral center to direct their attention toward key, strategic areas. The quality of that moral core will make all the difference. This is not a question of morality versus amorality or of one religion versus another, but an issue of how a leader's moral core is formed and how that core affects the manner in which he or she leads.

Everyone has a place in their character where values reside. Those values are formed from experiences that begin in childhood. As a person matures, those values coalesce around a central belief that sits at the heart of one's character. That belief is one that informs all others. Whether religious or secular in nature, that central belief is the lens through which all other values are focused and by which all other values are colored.[10] From those values, convictions arise — beliefs that form principles by which a person organizes one's life. Those convictions are the great organizing principles of effective political leaders.

Sarah Palin is not the first political candidate on the national scene to embody her beliefs through her actions and policies. History has offered glimpses of this integrity in past national leaders. Notably, Abraham Lincoln, Ronald Reagan, and Franklin Roosevelt all led from a well-defined moral center of strongly held beliefs. They used those beliefs to organize their efforts in office, focusing their time and attention on a few strategic areas. As a result, they presided over administrations that achieved significant goals and produced long-lasting benefits.

Abraham Lincoln had a firm belief that all people are created equal and that we dishonor God when we dishonor other races. He also believed that the unity of the states was necessary for the nation to survive. He paid a heavy price to uphold those strong convictions, but the result was a free and united country that arose in strength to become a world leader and is still striving for justice on behalf of the downtrodden.

Ronald Reagan was guided by a moral center that included a strong belief in God, firm commitment to individual liberty, and respect for free-market economics. From those core beliefs he developed a few, succinct governing objectives to which he held with almost obsessive devotion — reduce taxes, reduce the size of government, free small businesses from burdensome regulation, stand tough for the freedom and dignity of others. He didn't complete the work on all of those topics, but he left an indelible mark on the country.[11]

Franklin Roosevelt focused on an even shorter list — put the country back to work, provide the poor a hand up not a handout, and oppose tyranny at all costs.

When Roosevelt took office, 25 percent of the country's workforce was unemployed. To address that problem he began a number of programs designed to put people back to work. Combined with regulations for the securities and banking industries, the economy began to improve. Unemployment before World War II fell from 25 percent to 14 percent. He attained that goal by singularly focusing his efforts on a narrow set of objectives. Those objectives came from values that rested at the core of his character — namely a profound belief in the dignity and worth of persons.

At the end of the day, a leader's effect on the country will be a reflection of his or her basic values. History tells us of many who led by way of wrong values such as pride, hatred, greed, or a lust for power — all with devastating consequences for their country. It is impossible to overstate the importance of knowing what a leader really values.

At the center of Sarah Palin's moral core lies a profound belief in God, the Judeo-Christian God of Abraham, Isaac, and Jacob who is more fully revealed in the person and work of Jesus Christ. That belief arises from Sarah's personal spiritual insight, but it encompasses three main themes that inform all others: (1) a commitment to the truth and authority of Scripture, (2) a keen sense of justice, and (3) an ethic of personal responsibility.

Each of the churches Sarah has attended teaches and espouses a strong commitment to the truth and authority of Scripture. For Sarah, the Bible is not merely a book, but a record of God's revelation to humanity. An exchange reported in an issue of *International Herald Tribune* reveals the importance she assigns to Scripture.

Shortly after taking office as governor in 2006, Sarah Palin sent an e-mail message to Paul Riley, her former pastor in the Assembly of God Church, which her family began attending when she was young.

"She needed spiritual advice in how to do her new job," said Riley, who is 78 and retired from the church. "She asked for a Biblical example of people who were great leaders and what was the secret of their leadership," Riley said.

He wrote back that she should read again from the Old Testament the story of Esther, a beauty queen who became a real one, gaining the king's ear to avert the slaughter of the Jews and vanquish their enemies. When Esther is called to serve, God grants her a strength she never knew she had.[12]

From the opening chapters of Genesis, the first book of the Bible, Scripture describes a unique, symbiotic relationship between God, mankind, and creation. In that relationship, mankind is given the authority to exercise dominion and control over the earth. At the same time, mankind is placed in a dependent relationship with its environment. That tension — dominion yet dependence — is a relationship that has profound implications and one that has shaped Sarah's worldview, a worldview that reflects the same tension found in Scripture.

For instance, Sarah favors drilling in the Arctic National Wildlife Refuge,[13] one of several hot-button issues between Democrats and Republicans and one that sits at the center of the nation's energy policy. Although current efforts focus on development of only a small portion of that area, drilling is an environmentally invasive operation that would necessitate a human footprint in one of the nation's last untouched wilderness regions. A personal factor in this is that Sarah's husband is an employee of a major oil company and works in the oil fields of Alaska's North Slope.

Standing in contrast to her support for drilling in Alaska's wilderness, Sarah is an avid fan of hunting and is enthralled by the beauty and grandeur of Alaska's pristine wilderness. Sarah is equally well acquainted with the state's fishing industry. In addition to his work in the oil industry, Todd Palin is a part-time commercial fisherman in Bristol Bay, on the west side of the Alaska Peninsula.

When Todd and Sarah were first married, he employed her on his boat working a drift gill net in Bristol

Bay. This was not a lark on the water to fill a relaxing summer afternoon. Gill net fishing was hard work from an open boat Alaskans call a skiff. Unlike the light, shallow craft the name implies, an Alaskan skiff is a big heavy boat, twenty-five or thirty feet long with compartments in the bottom that can hold thousands of pounds of fish. When Sarah worked on the boat, she put in long hard hours of strenuous labor under less than pleasant conditions.[14] On one occasion she broke her hand while waiting to offload their catch to a tender boat. She had her hand tended to and returned the next day to continue working.[15]

Even though she was born in Idaho, Sarah has spent all but the first few months of her life immersed in Alaska's vast natural resources. The influence of that experience alone might have produced an ardent conservationist, but that was not the thing that most influenced her moral center. Her core beliefs formed around her faith in God and her view of Scripture.[16] Because of that, she came to see the earth and all its resources as the object of mankind's wise dominion; the earth is a thing to be developed, carefully managed, and used for the benefit of all, not merely to be set on a shelf for admiration.

When she discusses the topic as governor, Sarah often addresses the issue from a state constitutional perspective. Alaska was purchased from Russia shortly after the American Civil War and was later admitted to the Union primarily for the exploitation of its natural resources. The Alaska constitution contains provisions that address this historic fact and commit the state to that purpose.[17]

Speaking to a joint legislative assembly in her 2008 State of the State address, Governor Palin said,

> After our citizens, our state treasure is our commonly owned natural resources. Fifty years ago, our Constitution's founders established lofty goals and ironclad promises to be self-sufficient and self-determined through wise use of resources.[18]

While she addresses utilization of those resources from an historic and constitutional perspective, that policy fits well with her view of Scripture and the relationship of mankind to nature that Scripture portrays.

The tension in Sarah Palin's worldview is evident in other major issues she has faced. She is pro-life, both as a political position and as a personal lifestyle, yet she favors capital punishment. She is opposed to same-sex marriage but refused to endorse a measure that would have blocked state employee benefits to the partners of state employees engaged in same-sex relationships.

Rather than being a contradiction, she sees this tension in her worldview as creative and feels it reveals a dynamic aspect of her personality. Although she holds her core beliefs without wavering, that core is creative, not stagnant. Dynamic, not rigid.

American culture is growing and dynamic, changing at a pace that boggles the mind. The context in which we live is more fluid than any other in recent history. The issues we face this year—stem-cell research, the economy, nuclear arms, energy dependence—will come to us in a new context next year as new technology changes the available options and brings new moral dilemmas. Leaders in this century who are effective will have a worldview that can accommodate and assimilate an ever-changing context with inventive, innovative solutions.

If Scripture is her moral compass, Sarah's sense of justice is the needle. Blessed with an unwavering sense of what is right and wrong,[19] Sarah maintains a moral anchor that continues to steer her through the most challenging days of her political career. As one newsmagazine put it, "Friends say the Ten Commandments imbued her with a strong sense of right and wrong."[20]

While serving on the Alaska Oil and Gas Conservation Commission, Sarah was confronted with the option of looking the other way. In the scope of worldwide politics, no one would notice or care. Sarah, however, held to the beliefs that had guided her all her life, that right is right and wrong is wrong. Speaking of her at the time, Wayne Anthony Ross, a National Rifle Association board member, said, "It was a crisis of conscience for her.... Her personal integrity is very important to her, and here it appears she's behind a cover-up."[21]

Describing the moment herself, she said, "A good friend told me that in politics either you eat well or you sleep well.... I wasn't sleeping well."[22]

To know where that moral sense of "rightness" came from, one needn't look far. Sarah's experiences in family, church, and school were all built around duty, doing the right thing. In a home life that provided constant tutoring, with church as a focal point of her social interaction, it would be surprising if she had developed any other way.

Added to these qualities, Sarah has an unavoidable ethic of personal responsibility. She not only sees the way conditions are and how they could be better, but feels compelled to get involved, a sentiment she expressed from the very beginning of her political life. When told of her decision to enter the race for a seat on the city council, her father was confounded and responded by raising a question. "I said 'why?' and she just said, 'I feel like I can help the community.'"[23] And so has it been throughout her adult life.

From her first PTA meeting, Sarah was—as she said in her speech to the Republican National Convention —"just your average hockey mom, and signed up for the PTA because I wanted to make my kids' public education better."[24]

Commenting years earlier about her decision to run for mayor, she had said much the same thing. "I was on City Council for four years and I was making decisions, I was trying to help, but I realized then that in order to really set a tone and help set some direction and bring in what I thought the community needed, I needed … [to] get out of my comfort zone as one of many on the council and run for mayor."[25]

Beginning with no political ambition, Sarah Palin stepped out of the comfort zone of her own home and volunteered at her child's school. From there, she saw more that needed to be done, and her vision of her life began to grow. Rather than shrink back, she moved forward, being faithful to each opportunity that opened before her. At each new juncture she felt compelled to take the succeeding step.

In Sarah Palin one sees a person living from a fully integrated worldview. Her faith is not compartmentalized from the rest of her life. Faith. Family. Politics. Leadership. Together they form Palin's DNA. Take out any one strand, and the fabric unravels. Sarah's faith, her view of where she stands in relationship to God, would not be complete without political involvement. Her political involvement, campaigning for office and governing, would not be complete without the drive of her faith. The two are inextricably intertwined.

As the twenty-first century unfolds, leaders who lead effectively will possess a clear sense of True North. While not necessarily Christian, they will have an acknowledged sense of purpose that is completely integrated with their life and their approach to leadership. A worldview that encompasses every aspect of their life. A clearly defined sense of right and wrong. And a driving imperative of personal responsibility. In a century in which meaning is more often derived from relationship rather than from acceptance of unquestioned absolutes, perhaps no other leadership quality will be more important.

CHAPTER 5

MADE
IN THE USA

★

No one expects us to agree on everything.
But we are expected to govern with integrity,
good will, clear conviction, and a servant's heart.

Sarah Palin

Whether leading in business, education,
politics, or family, character always trumps charisma.
What we desperately need in our leaders today
is strong character.

Rick Warren

WHEN SARAH PALIN BURST ON THE NATIONAL SCENE THAT late-summer day in Dayton, Ohio, among the many labels pundits were quick to give her was that of populist.

In its historic context, the name refers to a grass-roots political movement of the late 1800s that began in the rural Midwest and South as an attempt to force government to address the plight of the nation's farmers. As momentum built for the cause, the movement became the Populist Party, which later merged with the Democrat Party.[1]

In political parlance, the term "populist" has since come to denote candidates with a broad voter appeal and a ground swell of grassroots support. Populist politicians typically advocate the cause of making government more responsive to the needs of citizens. Sarah

Palin believes this proposition and has spent her adult life pursuing the cause of making it a reality.

In each of her political campaigns, Sarah was underfunded and not always well versed in the issues. Yet, with a willing spirit and a low-budget approach—hard work and volunteer help—she found a way to improvise, adapt, overcome, and win. With hand-painted signs and flyers printed on a home computer, she reached out to voters with an authentic, genuine interest in the issues that affected their lives. Fueled and guided by a clearly defined sense of moral responsibility, and powered by values she had held for life—not just for the length of the campaign—she was swept into office with popular support not once, but five times: twice to the city council, twice to the office of mayor, and once to the office of governor.

Nothing captures the spirit of Sarah's approach, and the response she received, better than an incident that occurred during the 2006 gubernatorial campaign.

At one meeting with a group of trawlers and processors on Kodiak Island, Sarah listened but respectfully disagreed on a particular issue. Volunteer Frank Bailey recalled that before wrapping up the meeting she told the fishermen, "At this point I'll understand if you decide to support my opponent. Regardless of that, if I become governor I want you to know that I respect your views and will continue to listen to your concerns."

The next morning, back at Anchorage campaign headquarters, the fishermen's group called asking for two large eight-foot "Palin for Governor" signs to display in Kodiak. "We've decided to support Sarah because we believe she'll listen," the caller said.[2]

People responded with support to Sarah, even if they disagreed with her on the substantive issues, because they found in her something they sought that was bigger than their own self-interest: respect, honesty, and open communication. By any definition, this style embodies effective leadership.

Along with Sarah's fresh approach came a fresh response. In each of her elections, volunteers turned out in large numbers. During the 2006 campaign for governor, those volunteers swarmed over the state, handing out leaflets, sticking up yard signs, shaking hands, and talking to anyone who would listen to a few words about a candidate in whom they believed. More than any single issue, the election results turned on voter assessment of Sarah as a candidate rather than on her command of policy details.[3]

With candor and transparency, Sarah stayed true to what she is and who she is and who she has been throughout her political life—a hockey mom who is interested in making a difference. Voters heard that message and read it as a sign of honesty not seen in recent Alaska history. They trusted her and, as a result, voted for her in large numbers.

Still, nothing tests genuine authenticity quite like being confronted with an issue on which one finds no common ground. Sarah would face that challenge in her first year as governor.

✦

IN 1998, BEFORE SARAH PALIN ENTERED STATEWIDE politics, Alaska voters adopted an amendment to the state constitution: "To be valid or recognized in this state, a marriage may exist only between one man and one woman."[4] The measure had been designed and crafted by legislators opposed to same-sex marriage. Supported by many churches and other conservative organizations, the measure was ratified with little effective opposition.[5]

Sarah supported the amendment. Later, when campaigning for governor, she again made clear her opposition to gay marriage and reasserted her belief that marriage is a union reserved solely for heterosexual couples.[6] She holds this political position because of her belief in God and her view of Scripture, a conviction emanating from her moral core and informed by the reverence for heterosexual marriage in the Bible.

Within a month of her inauguration as governor, Sarah faced this issue head-on. The setting was not a theoretical debate or a quiet discussion around the kitchen table, but the real world of elected office.

When Alaskans adopted the constitutional amendment defining marriage in terms that excluded same-sex couples, a group of state employees living in same-sex relationships filed a lawsuit challenging the state's policy of denying benefits to their non-employee partners. A lower court upheld the policy and ruled in favor of the state. On appeal, the Alaska Supreme Court found that denying the benefits on the basis of sexual preference alone violated the state's constitutional provision guaranteeing equal protection.

In its ruling, the Alaska Supreme Court ordered the state to provide employee benefits to same-sex partners of state employees in a manner consistent with benefits provided to those in traditional marriages.[7] Many people in the state were outraged by the ruling, which seemed to contradict the recently adopted constitutional amendment designed to prevent the state from legally recognizing same-sex unions.[8]

In response to the court's order, the state legislature began work on a bill that was supposed to implement that ruling. Instead, led by outspoken critics and fueled by heated public sentiment against providing the benefits, the legislature crafted and passed a bill that prohibited the Alaska Department of Administration from promulgating rules and regulations necessary to put the court's order into effect. The legislature also passed a second bill, calling for a nonbinding statewide vote to gauge the opinion of Alaskans on the subject and to determine whether a constitutional amendment was necessary to prevent supplying the benefits.[9]

In reviewing the bill, the state attorney general informed Governor Palin that banning benefits under the proposed legislation was unconstitutional and would result in a protracted and costly legal dispute. Conservative legislators and leaders lobbied her to sign the measure into law, forcing a constitutional showdown between the judicial and executive branches of government.

The cost of litigation over the measure would have been significant, but that was not Sarah Palin's primary consideration. For her, the question of whether to sign the bill into law presented a tug-of-war between her personal opinion and core beliefs on the one hand, and her oath of office to uphold the state constitution on the other. In the end, Governor Palin exercised her first veto and blocked the legislation, effectively allowing the state to provide the benefits. As might be expected, opponents of same-sex unions were upset and focused their anger on the governor.[10]

Core values are essential in deciding how to govern and in determining the issues on which to focus, but that alone is not enough. Had Sarah Palin been guided solely by those values, she would have signed the bill into law the day it arrived on her desk. But values alone produce a demagogue, and Sarah has consistently refused to play such a role. Had she been merely interested in partisan politics, she would have acted otherwise. Instead, she gave the state and the nation a display of how politicians should handle issues that intersect their personal beliefs and their legal obligation.

In the past, politicians could avoid choosing between what they believed and the responsibility of their office by substituting partisan politics for genuine interest in the pressing issues of the day. Many people would not have noticed the difference. Sarah Palin could have adopted that strategy, sided with those who opposed gay marriage, and energized her voter base. For Sarah, however, those who favored a policy promoting and allowing benefits for same-sex unions were much like those fishermen on Kodiak Island: She didn't agree with them, but she was willing to listen.

In the end, Sarah vetoed the bill, not because she agreed with those who opposed it, but because she had taken an oath that obligated her to uphold the law. In her mind, the State Supreme Court was the arbiter of the law. Commenting on her action, she said, "Signing this bill would be in direct violation of my oath of office."[11] It was not an easy decision, and it ran contrary to much of what she had believed from childhood, but to her it was the right thing to do.

From a day early in the gubernatorial campaign when the question of her stance on same-sex unions had first been posed, Sarah had refused to judge those who engaged in a lifestyle with which she disagreed.[12] Also as governor, she refused to join in grandstanding litigation over it.[13] In doing that, she displayed the capacity to reach a decision on a polarizing issue that was thoughtful, reasoned, and tempered by a genuine interest in the lives of those around her.

The American culture demands leadership that provides an authentic message, that addresses the issues without dodging them and without casting unfavorable or disparaging facts in a light most favorable to that leader. Perhaps this is why the so-called "Troopergate" incident won't go away.

The underlying controversy centers on allegations that Sarah fired Walt Monegan, the public safety commissioner, because he wouldn't dismiss Mike Wooten, Sarah's former brother-in-law, who was an Alaskan state trooper.[14] Sarah's sister Molly had divorced Wooten, but a contentious custody dispute lingered. According to the allegations, members of Sarah's administration pressured Monegan to fire Wooten. When he refused,

Sarah fired Monegan. That's the story that has been reported.[15]

The issue really began when Monegan merely raised a question about whether the two might be related—his firing and the fact that Wooten remained on the trooper force. Monegan's question was all that Sarah's political opponents needed to get the ball rolling. Even then, the issue would have gone away except that after an initial denial, Sarah's own investigation revealed that some of her staff members, supposedly without her knowledge, had contacted Monegan about Wooten.

A denial followed by a revelation often gives the appearance that there may be more to a story than first supposed. In addition, Andrew Halcro, an independent candidate for governor whom Sarah defeated in 2006, devoted considerable attention to this story on his blog, which fed appetites for supposedly inside information.[16] Thus far, the end of the story hasn't been told. With Sarah's ascendency to the Republican presidential ticket, more scrutiny is guaranteed.

We live in an age in which voters demand authenticity. The demand for authenticity has been seen before in recent political history and is the reason "flip-flop" became the catch phrase of the 2004 Bush-Kerry election. During that campaign, Kerry changed positions on issues not once, but several times. He appeared to alter his position based not on well-reasoned grounds but solely on personal expediency and the desire to win. First he was in favor of continued funding for the war in Iraq, then he was against it. Later, in a statement explaining his votes, Kerry said "I actually did vote for the $87 billion before I voted against it."[17] After Republicans brought this and other changes in position to the public's attention, the label of "flip-flop" remained with Kerry for the rest of the campaign.

President Bush was similarly tagged with changes in position. During the 2000 campaign he indicated that same-sex marriage was not an issue the federal government needed to address. In 2004 he said it was.[18] Democrats, however, were never able to make the accusation stick against Bush because the presiding president, for all his inarticulate gaffs, connected with voters in a compelling manner. His response to the attacks by terrorists on September 11, his folksy appeal, and his penchant for addressing complex issues with simplifying rhetoric made him more appealing for many voters than Kerry's northeastern, staid public persona. Instead of fighting his limitations by attempting to be more than he was, Bush used those limitations to his advantage.

Ponderous, thoughtful contemplation of an issue guided by core values, using a reasoned decision process that leads to a change in position, is something people of this century will embrace. In fact, it is the kind of leadership for which they yearn. Changing positions merely to keep pace with the tide of partisan opinion, especially on issues that cannot be won through the governmental process, will be spotted as inauthentic and disingenuous.

For most of her political life, Sarah Palin has offered the same, unchanging message at each level of government. Government must pay for itself — self-sufficiency is not only an economic stance, but also a hallmark of Alaskan culture. Ethics in office is not an option — Sarah fought corruption at every level of office to which she was elected, even in her own party. Government should be about making life better for the people it was created to serve — not about lining the pockets of friends.

Speaking to friends and members of the press gathered at her home when she announced her gubernatorial campaign, Sarah said,

> Keeping it simple is my philosophy.... My desire is to see small, efficient government that's going to provide the basic services for Alaska, that's shared by the majority of Alaskans. And in keeping it simple, we know that Alaskans, we crave and we deserve leaders who are not going to approach all of our issues with just merely a partisan approach.[19]

Delivered in an honest, forthright, and plainspoken manner, Abraham Lincoln couldn't have said it better. The well-wishers and reporters gathered that day heard the same thing Wasilla voters had heard when Sarah first sought public office. Alaskans who listened to her during the failed run for the lieutenant governor's office had heard the message too. As chairman of the Alaska Oil and Gas Conservation Commission Sarah not only had stated that position, but also had lived by it. Even in the face of compelling pressure to do the opposite. It was a message that rose from deep inside her character and had defined her adult life.

And, in case anyone missed it, in her acceptance speech before the Republican National Convention in St. Paul, Minnesota, speaking to an audience that reached around the globe, Sarah said it once more.

> We are expected to govern with integrity, good will, clear convictions, and a servant's heart. I pledge to all Americans that I will carry myself in this spirit as vice president of the United States. This was the spirit that brought me to the governor's office, when I took on the old politics as usual in Juneau, when I stood up to the special interests, the lobbyists, big oil companies and the good-ol' boys network.
>
> Sudden and relentless reform never sits well with entrenched interests and power brokers. That's why true reform is so hard to achieve. But with the support of the citizens of Alaska, we shook things up.[20]

Sarah Palin has shown the nation how to energize a state through authentic, genuine interest in the issues that matter to constituents. She has also shown the mistakes one can make along the way. She is not perfect, but she is a glimmer, a hint of the authentic style of leadership necessary in an era drowning in information and moving forward at the speed of expediency.

CHAPTER 6

CHANGE CONSTANTLY

In politics, there are some candidates who use change
to promote their careers. And then there are those ...
who use their careers to promote change.

Sarah Palin

Change is inevitable.

Change is constant.

Benjamin Disraeli

WHEN SHE ENTERED OFFICE AS MAYOR OF WASILLA, Sarah Palin took control of a town in need of infrastructure. Increases in sales tax revenue produced by a growing, thriving local economy helped, but the town needed more improvements than it could purchase through its annual budget alone. In an effort to meet those needs, Sarah cast about for additional sources of support.

Using some of the city's limited funds, Sarah and the town council hired a lobbying firm. Not many towns with a population of 7,500 citizens hire lobbyists, but she thought it was worth the risk. She had campaigned on a message of "fresh faces and new ideas." Now it was time to put that concept to work.

With the lobbyist's help and with assistance from the Alaska congressional delegation, Sarah and the council secured more than $27 million in congressional appropriations for use on projects in the city and throughout the region. Some of the money went to improve sewers and streets and for a study to determine the feasibility of establishing a rail connection with the nearby city of Anchorage.[1] Local airport improvements and additional equipment for the police department also resulted from the funding. A large portion of the money went to a nonprofit transportation company that provided bus service in Wasilla.

Much of what counted as federal funding came in the form of loans rather than outright grants.[2] Obtaining federal help was a move that would become the subject of erroneous reports during Sarah's vice presidential campaign.[3] Although the $27 million she and the council obtained benefited the city, most of the money went to separate entities not under the direct control of the mayor or city government.

No one educated Sarah on how to operate a town. No one instructed her on the duties of mayor or how to maximize the town's financial resources. She had to educate herself and learn to adapt to constant change. With resiliency and resourcefulness, she consistently embraced the winds of change, unafraid to take chances to achieve the larger goal of improving the lives of her constituents.

In 2002, during Sarah's last year as mayor, the town of Wasilla voted to impose a half percent sales tax as a way to pay for a dream. For years, the citizens of Wasilla had been talking about a sports complex, but no one had been able to make it happen.

Sarah had no experience in floating bond issues to pay for improvements. She didn't know how to resolve title issues to property or foresee all the details necessary to plan and design a sports complex. But she found a way to make it happen. By improvising, adapting, and overcoming, she learned to embrace innovation and change, not simply to the services the town provided but to the way in which the town was governed.

As Sarah approached the end of her term, that sports complex was nearing reality. With a 102,000-square-foot arena, holding an ice sheet suitable for hockey, it was more than many had considered possible. Sarah's successor to the mayor's office, Diane Keller, stated, "It wouldn't have happened without Sarah."[4]

No longer a remote enclave, Wasilla was transforming itself into a suburb, a thriving, vibrant community to which people wanted to move to live and to rear their children. Sarah caught the pace of that change and rode it forward, in the process becoming an agent of the change that was already sweeping the region.

By the time she took office as governor, Sarah Palin had spent her entire political career improvising and overcoming. And she had done so without compromising her core beliefs. Her accomplishment is underscored by the hold large oil companies had on Alaska politics — a hold so deep and so corrupt that federal agents conducting an undercover investigation raided the offices of state legislators barely months before the 2006 fall elections.[5] Eventually, three current and former lawmakers were charged with taking bribes from an oil field services company.[6]

Instead of succumbing to the power wielded by the oil and gas industry, Governor Palin worked to find new ways of harnessing the resources for the good of citizens and not just the oil companies and their special interests. When Sarah was elected governor, one of the major issues dominating Alaska politics was the question of how to develop the state's vast natural gas reserves. First discovered in 1967, in and around Prudhoe Bay, proven reserves had since grown to include deposits beneath much of the northern portion of the state. The deposits were a natural resource with vast potential for Alaska and for consumers in the lower forty-eight states. Finding it was the easy part. Getting it to market had been a decades-long battle.

One proposal that garnered early support was a plan known as the All-Alaska Pipeline, a natural gas pipeline that would go across the state to a port along the Pacific coast.[7] From there the gas could be shipped south, presumably to ports in Washington and California. Alternative plans would have the pipeline traverse Canada, a more direct route to U.S. markets, but one that would require some $40 billion dollars in construction costs and the approval of the Canadian government.[8]

Sarah's predecessor, Frank Murkowski, succeeded in negotiating a deal with a consortium of oil companies led by BP that would lay the pipeline down the Canadian route. That plan included tax abatements and incentives that most found objectionable. Amid much opposition, and concerned that he would sign the contracts without their approval, the Alaska legislature filed a lawsuit against Murkowski seeking an injunction to prohibit him from going forward with the deal.[9] That injunction was still in place when Sarah became governor.

Faced with a complex challenge of immense proportion, newly elected Governor Palin did what she had done all her political life. She improvised, adapted, and overcame. First, she threw out the deal negotiated by Murkowski and scrapped state commitments to the project. Next, she gathered a staff capable of researching the options and began developing her own strategy. Favoring an approach that encouraged competition among private companies, the plan Sarah and her team developed became known as the Alaska Gasline Inducement Act—a plan that provided seed money from the state to any company or consortium willing to develop and operate a natural gas pipeline to deliver gas to the lower forty-eight states on a competitive basis under terms that benefited the people of Alaska.[10]

Not to be outdone, the oil companies with whom Murkowski had previously negotiated a tentative deal balked at the proposed plan and announced that, if passed, they would not participate in the new pipeline development. Sarah went ahead anyway, and when the plan was submitted to the legislature, all but one member voted in favor of it.[11]

Always moving forward, Sarah never met an obstacle she couldn't surmount. Searching for ways to improve the community where she lived, always trying to make things happen, she caught the spirit of the times perfectly and rode the crest of that wave to her destiny.

That same hope and possibility awaits all who are willing to risk the effort to step out and move nimbly with the times from one opportunity to the next. Leaders who can do that, who aren't afraid to take the risk of throwing away the play book, who are agile and constantly learning—those who can see the changing nature of relationships and who can find their way through obstacles without compromising their core beliefs—will be the leaders who take us through this century.

CHAPTER 7

FEAR IS
A FOUR-LETTER
WORD

★

I stood up to the special interests,
the lobbyists, big oil companies,
and the good-ol' boys network.

Sarah Palin

Take courage!
It is I. Don't be afraid.

Jesus of Nazareth

Sᴀʀᴀʜ Pᴀʟɪɴ's ᴇɴᴛʀʏ ɪɴᴛᴏ ᴛʜᴇ ʀᴀᴄᴇ ꜰᴏʀ ᴍᴀʏᴏʀ ᴏꜰ Wasilla in 1996, challenging three-term incumbent John Stein, was a bold move for a young woman in a small town. Yet Sarah prosecuted her bid with that energy and a fearless brand of spunk that would one day take her far beyond Alaska politics.

At one point in the campaign Sarah was offered a candidate's questionnaire prepared by the local newspaper. In her reply she cited a nonresponsive and rude city hall staff as one of the issues facing the community. She also noted that the current administration had a "tax and spend mentality." Answers to the questionnaire were published in the paper.

As one might expect, employees at city hall gave an equally invective response. In a letter also published in the paper, five city department heads stated,

If these allegations were true, and they most certainly are not, why does Ms. Palin, as a member of the city council, allow the practices to continue? Has she forgotten that it is the city council's responsibility to set policy and it is the administration's obligation to enforce that policy?[1]

And with that, the fight was on.[2]

Then, more so than now, Wasilla was not a large place. Within the boundaries of the city limits, there wasn't much room to hide. Unlike a large metropolitan city where one could presumably spend a lifetime and never see the same people twice, the people who live in Wasilla saw each other almost every day at the grocery store, the hockey game, the gas station. Candidates and city employees had little hope of avoiding each other. In addition, Sarah continued to serve on the city council, which made her presence at city hall a periodic necessity. Tensions began to rise.

Victoria Naegele, a resident of Wasilla, recalled of that first campaign, "It was just things you don't ever associate with a small town.... It was like we were warped into real politics instead of just 'Do you like Joe or Mary for the job?' It was a strange time."[3]

A fierce and resourceful competitor, Sarah waged a fight intent on achieving victory. To do that, she turned to issues that mattered most to her — infrastructure, new ideas, moving the town forward. She also found a way to interject larger, more divisive issues into the campaign — issues like abortion, term limits, and gun owner rights.[4]

Accustomed to a slower, gentler election climate, John Stein was taken aback. "Sarah comes in with all this ideological stuff, and I was like, 'Whoa,' ... But that got her elected: abortion, gun rights, term limits and the religious born-again thing."[5]

Once elected, Sarah began to make changes. Having campaigned on the need for fresh faces and new ideas, she started on that task as soon as she took office.[6]

To help bring about those changes, Sarah hired an outside attorney, paid with city funds, to advise her during the transition.[7] Then she hired a city manager to run day-to-day operations, an appointment that required her to rearrange the city budget to provide the position's salary.[8] The job had existed in the past but had gone unfilled for more than a year. Filling it almost certainly set tongues wagging at the Country Kitchen and elsewhere in the small town.

A few weeks after the election, Sarah asked for letters of resignation from the department heads who had endorsed the former mayor's bid for re-election.[9] Whether they saw it coming, no one seems to know. In Wasilla, most city employees serve at the pleasure of the mayor.[10]

Sarah wanted to make a new start with her own people, a decision she was authorized by law to make.[11]

Commenting on the transition years later, she said, "I learned you've got to be very discerning early on and decide if you can win them over or not. If you can't, you replace them early on."[12]

As complaints mounted about the changes she had made, and as articles appeared in the newspaper, Sarah issued an order prohibiting employees from talking to the press about city business without her approval.[13]

In response to the mayor's request for letters of resignation, the chief of police refused, citing a contract he had signed with the previous mayor.[14] Eventually, Sarah accepted the resignation of the museum director and eliminated the position. Before long, several others quit. Not long after that, though facing the possibility of a lawsuit over the contract he had signed, she fired the chief of police.[15]

Within a few short weeks, disgruntled Wasilla residents got together to discuss the things that had happened at city hall.[16] With town gossip fanning the flames of discontentment and the local newspaper adding negative editorials, disgruntled employees and a few others began to whisper about an effort to oust Sarah from office with a recall vote.[17] Meetings were held. People shouted and fumed and said what they thought about their new mayor. But in the end, nothing came of it.[18]

Before things calmed down at city hall, Sarah fired the librarian, Mary Ellen Emmons. Subsequent news reports during her campaign for vice president raised the allegation that Emmons was fired because she refused to ban books from the library. Reports of the incident written at the time Emmons was fired give no reason for her dismissal. From related events, it appears she was fired because of her public support for Stein during the campaign.[19] The reaction of the community to that decision was more widespread than the reaction to some of the other firings Sarah had made. In a rare move, Sarah recanted and gave Ms. Emmons back her job.[20]

Through it all, Sarah seems to have never flinched. Instead, she stayed on course and stuck to her goal of reducing taxes, cutting waste, building infrastructure, and improving the town with new and innovative ideas. Guided by what she determined to be right and wrong, she moved forward and took the town with her. It was an exercise she would repeat more than once in the future.

★

WHAT SEEMED LIKE THE END OF HER CAREER, IN reality, was a strategic turn toward the fulfillment of her destiny. Fear would have invited Sarah to yield to the circumstances that faced her. Had she done so, she would have been relegated to political obscurity. If she had accommodated the corruption around her and allowed it to continue unexposed, she would have lost all moral authority. Not only that, but she would have been forever beholden to those who engaged in that corruption and would have lived the remainder of her life wondering at which moment they were going to suddenly reveal her complicity in the unethical conduct. Instead, she gave fear no quarter and pressed ahead.

In 2005, Sarah crossed party lines to join Democratic State Representative Eric Croft in filing an ethics complaint against Gregg Renkes, the attorney general.[21] The allegations stemmed from an international coal deal that involved a company in which Renkes owned stock.

According to the allegations, Renkes, working on behalf of Governor Murkowski and the State of Alaska, helped negotiate a deal between the state, a Taiwanese company, and a Denver company named KFx, to develop a coal field east of Anchorage. Coal in those deposits was too high in moisture to be of commercial use. KFx supposedly had developed a drying process that would convert it to useable quality. Renkes owned stock in KFx at the time he negotiated the transaction.[22]

Renkes, a man many found to be a bright light in the Murkowski administration,[23] had been appointed to the attorney general position, but he wasn't just any political appointee. Before accepting the post, he had worked as Murkowski's aide and was his former campaign manager. He was the man most instrumental in getting Murkowski elected to the governor's office.[24]

As facts about Renkes's stock ownership came to light, Croft and others complained about the matter. In response, Murkowski asked U.S. Attorney Robert Bundy to investigate.[25] When Bundy issued a ruling that found some problems but declared that Renkes's interest in the company was insufficient to require punitive action, Murkowski issued Renkes a letter of reprimand. Incensed by what he felt was a weak reproof, Croft filed a formal ethics complaint. He asked Sarah to join him to give the complaint an appearance of having bipartisan support.[26]

If she was an outcast before, joining a Democrat in filing a complaint against a member of her own party made Sarah the enemy. This time, however, she was free of the secrecy restrictions that accompanied the investigation — limitations that had forced her to keep quiet before about the case against Randy Ruedrich.

Sarah, though no longer supported by those who controlled the state Republican Party, had survived, and her reputation with Alaska voters as an anti-corruption maverick was quickly becoming legendary. That reputation gave her the momentum she needed to consider returning to the statewide electoral politics.[27]

In 2006 Sarah entered the Republican primary as a

candidate for governor against the incumbent, Frank Murkowski. Running against a sitting governor meant competing against the state Republican Party machine. The primary contest proved a tough battle, but her public persona as an anti-corruption candidate made her the perfect candidate at the perfect time. She knew she faced a formidable opponent, yet she wasn't afraid.

In order to succeed in our new millennium, a politician must display consistency, courage, and candor when confronted with both new opportunities as well as old challenges. By acting decisively, embracing change, and seizing opportunities despite the obstacles, Sarah Palin has proven herself to be such a leader.

CHAPTER 8

WORK IS A LIFESTYLE

My Mom and Dad both worked at the elementary school in our small town. And among the many things I owe them is one simple lesson: that this is America, and every woman can walk through every door of opportunity.

Sarah Palin

Whatever you do,
work at it with all your heart.

Paul of Tarsus

As a junior at Wasilla High School in 1981, Sarah Palin competed as a member of the girl's basketball team and a distance runner on the girl's track and field team. Her father, who taught science and coached the track team, didn't think she was a talented runner but admired her perseverance.

"I look back on Sarah's perseverance," he says, "and whatever she wanted to do, she put her nose to the grindstone, especially in sports. If she didn't have a certain ability, she worked and worked and worked until she obtained that ability or skill."[1]

Although not gifted with raw athletic ability like others on the team, Sarah always found a way to win.[2] Her father says, "I had a bunch of good girls, a bunch of good runners, and she [Sarah] was just mediocre in practice.... At the first meet, she smoked everyone, and that opened my eyes, and the competitiveness in her really came out that day."[3]

When the basketball season opened that year, Sarah began as a player on the varsity team. Working hard, she gained only limited playing time. A number of the girls on the team were seniors, and the squad was loaded with talent. Sarah was forced to spend much of the early games that year waiting her turn and watching from the bench. When she complained to the coach, he asked her to play with the junior varsity, a team of mostly younger girls who were working hard but still needed to improve. Sarah was upset with the suggestion that she "play down" that year, but she did it anyway and finished the season with the second squad.[4]

That year, the varsity team qualified for the state basketball championship playoffs. Angry and upset that she was excluded, Sarah watched from the stands as the team came close to a championship, but eventually lost.[5]

The next year, when Sarah was a senior, proved that her time spent playing with the junior varsity had paid off. Through hard work and devotion her skill had improved. Moreover, spending time as an older member on a team composed of girls who were mostly younger had sharpened her confidence in her ability to lead. With the varsity, she was starting point guard and co-captain of the team.[6]

Chris Boese, who played against her in high school, commenting on an article about Sarah, said, "It talked about how her competitiveness as a high school basketball player brought her on this path [of politics]. As somebody who often had the job of guarding Sarah Heath, point guard to point guard, I can vouch for that."[7]

Don Teeguarden, the team coach, remembers Sarah as a leader. "She was a starting player ... a good leader, a good competitor.... She was a real integral part of the success of that team."[8]

With hard work and determination, Sarah and her team again had a winning record in that senior year. But in a game near the end of the season, Sarah hurt her ankle. Although the team once again qualified for the girl's state basketball championship playoffs, Sarah was nursing an injury. When the pain persisted, her parents took her to the doctor.[9] Her father remembers, "The doctor said, 'Yeah, you've got a bad sprain,' so we immobilized [her ankle] and he said, 'It's up to her,' so we let her play."[10]

The final game of the playoffs was against Robert Service High School, an Anchorage school of some two thousand students.[11] Wasilla was much smaller. Surely, it must have seemed, David never met a giant quite as big as the one they did.[12] To Wasilla's advantage, the game was played in the gymnasium at Wasilla High

School before a packed house of wildly supportive fans. No one gave the home team much of a chance, but most of the town turned out to see them try.[13]

Through the first two quarters the game was nip and tuck. Wasilla, playing over its head, kept pace with Service High point for point. Sarah, working hard and playing in her scrappy style, put forth an unusual effort in her determination to leave nothing in the locker room. Still hampered by the ankle injury, she had limited mobility and finally was forced to sit out most of the second half.[14]

From the bench Sarah watched as her teammates battled back and forth, moving up and down the court. Near the end of the fourth quarter, with the game tied and the team looking tired, Coach Teeguarden glanced down the bench. Perhaps it was compassion, seeing his senior player relegated to the role of spectator, or perhaps it was brilliant strategy, but what happened next became a story the town remembers to this day.[15]

With the score tied and the game on the line, Teegaurden sent Sarah back into the game. She had worked hard all four years, improved herself, and attained a level of skill no one thought she would be able to reach. And she was co-captain of the team. If anyone deserved to be on the floor at the end of the game, she did.[16]

On the inbounds pass, Sarah took the ball and moved up the court toward the goal. The pounding of the ball against the wood floor was barely audible even to herself above the din of noise rising from the crowd. Everyone was on their feet, waiting to see how the game would turn out.[17]

Sarah dribbled the ball, her feet moving quickly from side to side as she jockeyed for position to get past the Robert Service defense. Rubber soles on her shoes squeaked against the shiny smooth surface of the floor. As she ducked her shoulder to get past a player, the whistle sounded, stopping play. A referee, watching from a few feet away, had called a foul against the Robert Service team. There were ten seconds on the clock.[18]

The Wasilla team rallied around Sarah with words of encouragement and escorted her toward the free-throw line. When they reached the end of the court, they spread out and took their places along the lane beneath the basket. Sarah took her place at the line and looked up.[19]

To the left and right, the crowd stomped their feet and shouted, some hoping she would make the shot, others hoping she would miss. The referee checked the alignment of the opposing teams, glanced over at Sarah, and tossed her the ball.[20]

The orange leather felt comfortable to her hand as Sarah gripped it with her fingers. She had worked all her young life for this moment. Now it came down to a few final seconds. With cool, deliberate ease, she bounced the ball against the floor. Once. Twice. Three times. Then she rested it against the flat of her hand.[21] As she had a thousand times before, she bent her arm at the elbow and positioned the ball just beneath her chin. Bending her knees, she squatted slightly, then pushed through with her legs and extended her arm. The ball slipped from her hand and traveled in a smooth arc toward the round steel hoop. All eyes watched to see where it would land. From the feel of it as the shot slipped off her fingertips, Sarah already knew where it was headed.[22]

When the ball reached the top of its trajectory, it turned downward and sailed toward the backboard. With a swish, it dropped through the hoop and bounced to the floor. The crowd went wild. A second shot sealed the game as an announcer shouted, "Sarah's shot is there! She's aced the game for the Wasilla warriors!"[23] When the horn sounded to end play, they were the new state champions.[24]

That game was a success that Sarah would later describe as a life-changing moment.[25] Not so much because the team won the championship, but because she experienced firsthand how hard work can unleash immeasurable potential. With determination and single-minded devotion, she and her teammates accomplished far more than their raw talent, unchallenged by the rigors of hard work, would have allowed.

In the course of that season, Sarah earned the nickname "Sarah Barracuda" for her fierce, competitive play. Another of her coaches, Roger Nelles, said, "The name probably fit her because of that intensity. She led by example. She's diving on the floor, she's playing tough defense...."[26] It was a nickname that would follow Sarah into adulthood, a nickname that described a trait many had already seen in her personality—a stubborn, unbending determination. Once convinced she was right, Sarah would not stop until she prevailed.[27]

Remembering the championship experience during her 1996 mayoral campaign, Sarah told a reporter from the *Anchorage Daily News*, "This really sounds hokey, but that was a turning point in my life," she said. "We were supposed to be the underdogs big time. You see firsthand anything is possible and learn it takes tenacity, hard work, and guts."[28]

★

THE ATTITUDE THAT SARAH HEATH DISPLAYED DURING track meets and on the basketball court was one she had learned at home. Living simply but comfortably, the family learned to work hard to produce the things they needed. Their home was heated by a wood stove, which meant someone had to cut and stack the wood, then bring it into the house and stoke the fire. That task fell to Sarah and her siblings.[29]

For food the Heaths relied heavily on wild fish and game caught and killed by Sarah's father. At mealtime, fresh moose and caribou from the freezer was supplemented with vegetables grown in a large garden. As children, Sarah and her sisters and brother learned to live from the fruit of their labors. Learning the lesson that food comes to the table as a result of hard work made them appreciate the value of their work. Mr. and Mrs. Heath made sure that Sarah understood that lesson well.[30]

Trudging over Alaska's rough terrain with a rifle on her shoulder, Sarah learned the joy of a life outdoors and the thrill of a successful hunt. (She is a longtime member of the National Rifle Association.)[31] Many mornings during her high school years, Sarah's father, an avid hunter and fisherman, awakened her long before dawn so she could accompany him on a morning moose hunt. When former U.S. Senator Fred Thompson suggested she was the only candidate for vice president who could field-dress a moose,[32] he was probably right. Sarah knew how to find them, shoot them, and pack them out. No mean accomplishment for a high school student, female or male.[33]

☆

WHILE SARAH'S PARENTS WERE TEACHING HER TO WORK, they were also teaching her to learn. Learning was a lifestyle modeled in their home. With a school teacher for a father and a school secretary for a mother, Sarah was constantly encouraged to learn. Her father, a science teacher, not only hunted and fished for wild game to feed the family, but studied the animals as well, filling their home with samples of animal hides, bones, and fossils.[34]

At an early age, Sarah fell in love with the newspaper and read it from beginning to end, devouring and digesting every bit of news. Reminiscing about her childhood, her father said, "... she read the newspaper more than I did. I'd grab the sports; she'd grab the front page—I remember that distinctly ... and she would read all of it, all the national part and the local part. And I'd look at the headlines; she'd read it all through."[35]

That love of learning and exposure to a broad range of subjects served Sarah well as she entered political life. On the city council and later as mayor, she was confronted by issues that were new and challenging. A quick study, she learned enough about the issues the town faced to make an informed decision.

When Sarah moved from councilwoman and two-term mayor to chairman of the Alaska Oil and Gas Conservation Commission, she had to learn about the oil and gas business. A complex business that encompasses a number of specialties, oil and gas are the state's most valuable natural resources. Sarah had to study hard and learn fast. Her job on the commission gave her the responsibility of overseeing the development of those treasures. As chairman, she had to learn quickly not only the underlying nature of the business, but also the manner in which the commission functioned.

When she became governor, Sarah stepped up to an even more complex role with even broader implications.

At each step of the way, Sarah applied the skill of hard work and a lifelong love of learning to equip herself to do the job at hand. She was faithful to discharge her duties at each new level of increasing responsibility and did her best to do a good job. That was something she had been doing all her life. Even though she wasn't an expert in any one field, she nevertheless attained the requisite knowledge to make good decisions.

In an era dominated by a rising tide of information and data, Sarah's skills of hard work and love of learning equipped her well for service. With hard work and a willingness to learn, she was able to sort through the growing volume of information that confronted her in order for her to make good decisions. Her resolve to use those skills and apply them to the challenges she faced pointed her toward greater and greater success as she matured and grew as a leader.

This approach of constantly learning is a style demanded by the age in which we live. With information growing at an incalculable rate, no one can hold command of every detail in every discipline. Leaders who are effective will develop familiarity with a wide range of subjects rather than a depth of detail in a few. By developing a working knowledge covering a wide range of subjects, leaders will be free to rise above individual issues to see the whole picture—the manner in which the issues are related, and the comparative value of each issue.

CHAPTER 9

MEAN IT
LIKE YOU SAY IT

★

And children with special needs
inspire a special love.
Sarah Palin

You can preach a better sermon
with your life than with your lips.

Oliver Goldsmith

IN DECEMBER 2007, GOVERNOR SARAH PALIN WAS FOUR months pregnant. As a routine matter, her physician ordered an amniocentesis. As a prenatal test of cells in the amniotic fluid around an unborn child, amniocentesis is reliable and effective in detecting birth defects. It is a test routinely ordered for women who become pregnant after the age of thirty-five. Sarah was forty-three.[1]

When her physician called to give her the results, Sarah knew from the tone of his voice that the results were serious. "You need to come to the office so we can talk about it."[2]

Sarah insisted on hearing the news right then. Reluctantly, the doctor uttered the words, "Down syndrome."[3]

Those two words confronted Sarah with another life-changing moment. A strong pro-life advocate,

Sarah had consistently opposed abortion. She had made that stance known to her friends, she had repeated it in church, and she had mentioned it in the course of her several political campaigns. It was and is one of her core beliefs—a value that lies at the very heart of who she is and how she views the world. Now she was faced with a situation that posed a potential challenge to the resolve of that position.[4]

In the United States, thousands of pregnant women each year undergo prenatal tests similar to the one Sarah Palin received. Of those women who are found to be carrying a child with Down syndrome, almost 90 percent choose to have an abortion rather than carrying the child to term.[5] Although they might have been disappointed by her decision, many women would have understood if Sarah had made that choice too. But for Sarah there was never any doubt. She was going to have the baby. She was pro-life in theory and pro-life in practice. In spite of the challenges that lay ahead for herself and her family, she refused to make an exception for her own circumstances, she refused to abandon her beliefs, and she refused to abandon the child growing inside her body.[6]

Living what you believe, even when no one is looking, isn't always easy. It has been said, "The real test isn't how you act in public, it's how you act when no one's around." Those words were never more true than on that day when Sarah and her family received the news about their baby. Sarah believed her family was important and she meant it, even when the consequences fell in hard and difficult ways. That applied not only to questions about pregnancy and birth. It applied to other matters as well. An outstanding example of this is the way she let go of a chance to become a senator out of consideration for her older son's needs.

In 2004, Lisa Murkowski was up for re-election to the U.S. Senate seat to which her father had appointed her, a Senate seat Sarah Palin still wanted. Friends and political supporters encouraged her to run. Long a source of help, her circle of support ranged from well-intentioned cheerleaders to serious-minded facilitators ready to raise campaign dollars and make things happen.[7]

Sarah had wanted that Senate seat in 2002 when she had worked hard to get Frank Murkowski elected governor. Her political instincts told her it should have been hers back then. She was certain Murkowski had made a big mistake in appointing his own daughter instead. In that opinion she was not alone.[8] Sarah wanted to run in that upcoming election, but she had to clear one crucial hurdle.[9]

Moving to Washington, D.C., would mean a huge disruption in the Palin family's life. In Wasilla they lived near grandparents, aunts, uncles, and cousins. They had friends there, and their roots ran deep in the community. Todd's ancestors had lived in Alaska for as long as the state had been inhabited by humans. Moving across the continent to the nation's capital would take their lives in an entirely new direction. If Sarah was going to enter the Senate race, she needed everyone to agree. The family would have to back her. Unanimously.[10]

When Sarah polled the family, all were in favor of joining the campaign—everyone except Track, her oldest. Already a teenager and well into high school, he wanted to stay in Wasilla and finish with his class. He also had seen the inside of enough campaigns to know that this one would be rough. He insisted that his mother not expose the family to public scrutiny.[11]

Nevertheless, Sarah wanted to beat Lisa Murkowski and claim that Senate seat. Sarah knew what the people of Alaska needed, but she was not in a position to do anything about it. She wanted to make things happen—that had been her nature since early childhood—but she couldn't do it without her family's approval, cooperation, and agreement to the mission.[12]

So when Track voiced his dissent, Sarah backed down. It was not an easy thing for her to do, but she stepped away from the campaign and trusted that everything would work for the best.[13] Relying on her belief in God and her core values, which include a strong commitment to her family, she trusted that he would guide her to her destiny, no matter how circuitous the route might seem.[14]

✯

IN ADDITION TO HER COMMITMENT TO FAMILY AND HER public stance opposing abortion, Sarah had been an advocate for a strong national defense. It is an issue that has roots in Alaska's history.

At several points along its coastline, Alaska sits less than a hundred miles from Russia. Not only that, but it is the only portion of North America invaded by the Japanese during World War II. Three of the Aleutian Islands were occupied by Japanese troops. They remained there for more than a year, and dislodging them required a special military operation. In response, the United States established military bases there to guard and protect that region from future incursions. Military bases located in Alaska make a significant contribution to the country's national defense and to the state's economy.

Before she was elected governor, Sarah favored opposing terrorism wherever it is found and supported the deployment of troops to the Middle East and the war in Iraq. When units from the Alaska National Guard deployed to Iraq, she traveled as far as Kuwait to visit them.

Sarah favored those policies when she lived comfortably in Alaska and trouble was a long distance away. And she favored it on September 11, 2007, when her son,

Track, enlisted with a friend in the United States Army. In September 2008, just days after Sarah accepted the Republican nomination for vice president, Track deployed with his unit to Iraq. After a brief stopover in Kuwait to become accustomed to the climate, he will be stationed in Iraq for a year.[15]

Referring to her running mate, John McCain, during her remarks to the Republican National Convention, Sarah said, "As the mother of one of those troops, that is exactly the kind of man I want as commander in chief. I'm just one of many moms who'll say an extra prayer each night for our sons and daughters going into harm's way."[16] More than campaign rhetoric, her words carry with them an invocation of blessing and protection for her son.

Sarah's belief in life and family faced one more challenge. In the days leading up to her appearance before the Republican National Convention, the McCain-Palin Campaign announced that Sarah's oldest daughter, Bristol, was pregnant. News of the unmarried teen's pregnancy came at an awkward moment.

In a prior era, some politicians might have sent their daughter away to have the baby quietly out of the glaring eye of news photographers and television cameras. Or they might have declined the invitation, fearful of public scrutiny and judgment on their family. Instead of dodging the issue, the Palins faced it head-on.[17]

The timing of the announcement was spurred, perhaps, by rumors circulating on Internet websites suggesting Trig really was Bristol's child, not Sarah's. Rumors often take a life of their own, and when the one about Trig wouldn't go away, the Palins decided to announce the truth. Back home in Wasilla, most people already knew about it. Anyone who wanted to know the details could easily find them out. The world might as well know the truth too.[18]

In a written announcement the Palins said, "Our beautiful daughter Bristol came to us with news that as parents we knew would make her grow up faster than we had ever planned. As Bristol faces the responsibilities of adulthood, she knows she has our unconditional love and support."[19]

Although disappointed, Sarah and Todd did not shrink back from the issues they faced. Instead, they clung to their core values and faced difficulty with the same resolve with which they had faced challenges before. No nation could ask more of a leader than that she face the issues of her private life with the same standard and vision she offers to the country. Sarah Palin meant it when she said she was pro-life, pro-national defense, and pro-family. She meant it when she said it, and she continues to live it that way.

Mean it like you say it. The age in which we live cries out for transparent leadership. Leaders who hold the same policy positions in private that they do in public. Who live by the same standard they seek to impose on the people whom they serve, even when that standard falls in uncomfortable and unpleasant places.

CHAPTER 10

MOTHER KNOWS BEST

★

Our family has the same ups and downs as any other,
the same challenges and the same joys.
Sometimes the greatest joys bring challenge.

Sarah Palin

She brings him good,
not harm, all the days of her life

Proverbs 31:12

THREE DAYS AFTER TRIG WAS BORN, SARAH PALIN entered the governor's office with him wrapped safely in her arms. When asked whether she could manage the duties of her office and care for her new baby with special needs, she gave a quick and incisive response. "I can think of so many male candidates who watched their families grow while they were in office. There is no reason to believe a woman can't do it with a growing family."[1]

When Governor Palin made those comments in Alaska, not too many people outside the state noticed. However, when she was introduced as John McCain's running mate, the size of her family—five children— and the fact that her infant had Down syndrome set off a stormy debate over the role of women in the workplace and, more particularly, women in executive positions.

Oddly enough, the majority of those who raised this issue as a challenge to Sarah's suitability for the vice presidency were Democrats, the group that had led the decades-long fight in favor of breaking down barriers that had traditionally prohibited women from attaining those positions.

Mothers all across the country juggle children and family responsibilities to accommodate a busy lifestyle. In the process, they make decisions about whether to repair the car or buy their children a new pair of shoes, wondering all the while how much more they can squeeze from the grocery budget. Running the household is a full-time job and requires at least as much energy as the job that provides a paycheck. In the process, mothers learn valuable skills that often prepare them far better for leadership roles than do the experiences of their male counterparts.[2]

In many respects, Sarah Palin matured as a leader in government as she matured in parenting. Her entry into politics was not a later-in-life decision, nor was her decision to have a family. Like most things she attempted, she did them all at once. Leadership is leadership—the fact that one is a household and the other a state, or even a country, makes little difference. The skills to do either job are much the same. Only the scale and scope differ.

Having been a brash, almost cocky, young member of the city council, Sarah thought she could do the job of mayor. When she arrived, she was bent on making things different. One of her first acts as mayor of Wasilla was to ask for resignations, and then she began dismissing employees. Her actions were seen by others as unwarranted, if not reckless. Later, as she survived to serve a second term, she harnessed that reckless energy and made it work to her benefit.

In talking about Sarah's style of leadership, Donald Moore, at the time the Mat-Su Borough[3] manager, said,

> Sarah's governance is consensus oriented.... She makes sure everyone has a chance to have a say; nobody gets left out. But there comes a point when the debate is over and a decision has to be made. She's also the type of manager that once she reaches her cadence, she expects everyone to keep up.[4]

Diane Keller, who served on the city council while Sarah was mayor and later succeeded her in that office, said the same thing: "She was a consensus builder."[5]

Through trial and error, Sarah learned to lead. No doubt, parenting reinforced that process. It also taught her to pick her battles and to negotiate openly and willingly from a position of strength without concern that others might think she was weak. As the person in charge, she could take confidence in her authority. Because she had the last word, she was free to be transparent and to conduct business without the cloak of secrecy. Even beyond the positions of councilwoman and mayor, Sarah's work as governor gave her ample opportunity to put that ability to the test.

One of the major issues that put Sarah to the test was that plan for the All-Alaska Pipeline that was still on hold by legal injunction when she became governor. She needed to come up with a more workable and ethical alternative from the one proposed by her predecessor, but opponents during the election campaign contended that she was not well enough informed about the matter and lacked the business acumen to handle such a complex issue. In response, the new governor and her staff put together a legislative proposal, called the Alaska Gasline Inducement Act, that would have the state front up to $500 million in development costs to a company willing to construct and operate a natural gas line on a direct route across Alaska and Canada and into the lower forty-eight states. Gaining approval from the Alaska legislature for the measure that would authorize the project was no easy feat. When she presented the measure, she was met with opposition from several large oil companies who had a competing plan and from some self-interested legislators. The bill stalled. But it passed on the last day of the legislature's session.[6]

Guiding that bill from concept to reality required attention to numerous details. It also required a guiding hand and a willingness to listen and compromise.

Referring to the bill afterward, State Representative Mike Doogan said, "AGIA got caught up in the end-of-sessions shenanigans, but finally passed in much the form Palin wanted."[7] "Much the form": not exactly, but close enough. An ability to negotiate, to give up a detail without giving up the goal, is a crucial skill of an effective governor. (It is also a crucial skill of effective mothering.)

Once the bill was approved and signed into law, the governor and her staff were prepared to find a private company to partner with the state in building a gas line. To do that, they began negotiating with potential companies. As the process began, Sarah favored an open and transparent approach. That decision met with criticism. In an editorial published in the *Anchorage Daily News*, Dan Fagan wrote, "Openness and transparency isn't all it's cut out to be...."[8] Still, Governor Palin stuck to her position and insisted on dealing up front with potential partners. Backroom deals had marked Alaskan politics too long. Decisions of that nature were the sort of thing she had resisted and campaigned against throughout her political career. In August 2008, those open and transparent negotiations produced an agreement between the state of Alaska and TransCanada to begin work on permitting the new pipeline.[9] How did Sarah accomplish that? Through honesty, transparency, and an ability to choose the issues worth fighting for and those to let go of. Through critical skills for effective negotiation. Through critical skills learned and sharpened as a parent.

Bringing her children to the office was not something Sarah Palin did for the first time as governor. When she was mayor of Wasilla, she often brought her youngest child, Piper, to city hall. Like many other couples, Sarah and her husband learned to coordinate their schedules and share household responsibilities. Sarah had gifts, talents, and an interest in serving. Staying at home merely for the sake of tradition would have forfeited a lifetime of learning. Together she and her husband found ways not only to cope but, even better, to broaden and enrich the lives of their children by involving them in a life of service to others.

"Sometimes the kids would come with me." Sarah said. "Other times, since we lived just a couple of miles away, I went home to nurse the baby. It all worked out—I just let people know I had a family."[10]

Sarah also had the option of leaving the children at home when her schedule required.[11] "I am thankful to be married to a man who loves being a dad as much as I love being a mom, so he is my strength."

If anything about Sarah's life is clear, it is that she knows her own mind well. She has been guided throughout her life by a sense of honesty, confidence, and an eagerness to get involved. As her life continues to unfold, that will doubtless be the same.

For Sarah Palin, the lines between family, work, and play do not really exist. She brings her kids with her on trips and to the office, often with her husband coming along too. Juneau holds the distinction of being the only state capital in the United States that is not accessible by road. As a result, Sarah has tended to be a governor on the move, living much of the time in her own home. Finding her at the state fair or walking along the street on a pleasant Saturday morning has not been uncommon. Much of their life revolves around work, family, and church.

In an age of supposed sophistication, the Palin family is a throwback to a different time, when everyone worked together to provide food to eat and to keep the home warm while taking pleasure in the outdoors. Sarah's life has been that way since childhood. Although she now has no basic need to garden for essential vegetables, hunt moose to feed her family, or stack wood to keep the house warm, she still does these things. And she, no doubt, is passing that lifestyle on to her children, if not by necessity, at least by example. No one could hope to do more.

Throughout her political career Sarah confronted the issue of gender and the bias much of the American culture still holds against women. Many of the challenges to her credentials for office, lack of experience, or lack of knowledge in a particular field were not-so-subtle attacks targeted solely on the fact that she is female. As the United States moves forward in this century, leadership positions will become increasingly open to women. Perhaps American culture at large might even embrace the unique perspective and qualities women bring to leadership roles.

In this century Americans will be forced to face not only the questions of gender bias, but the underlying issue of how leadership transcends gender. Those who succeed in being effective leaders will not shrink from this task.

CHAPTER 11

LEADERSHIP ISN'T A BEAUTY CONTEST

I'm not going to Washington to seek
their good opinion — I'm going to Washington
to serve the people of this country.
Sarah Palin

In those days, of course,
we didn't have exit polls.

Sam Donaldson

IN MODERN POLITICAL LIFE, MANY CANDIDATES AND elected officials turn to polls for guidance. Often operating in the vacuous environment of a capital city, they feel the need to gauge public sentiment. Like a baker opening the door of the oven, they want to see how the cake is rising. They want to know what people are thinking. Harry Truman was not that kind of politician. Speaking of polls he once said,

> I have no more confidence in polls than I had before the [1948] election.... I never did have any confidence in polls, and I haven't got any confidence now. I make my decisions on whether it's right or wrong from my point of view, and after I have all the information and all the facts I can get to go on. Polls have no effect on me whatever.[1]

Sarah Palin could have used that quote for a press release.

When Sarah came to the governor's office in 2006, she inherited an office imbued by the state constitution with considerable power. "Alaskan governors can edit legislation, and their vetoes are tougher for lawmakers to overcome."[2] She had the power. The only issue remaining was how to use it.

Facing Sarah that first year was a large and expensive project known as the "Bridge to Nowhere." With enormous costs entailed, Sarah had to decide whether to go forward with construction or end it.

Coined by Keith Ashdown, a lobbyist for Taxpayers for Common Sense, the term "Bridge to Nowhere" was a catchy phrase that summed up popular opinion regarding excessive preferential spending.[3] Ashdown invented the phrase so that people would remember the issue of excessive preferential spending — or more familiarly, "pork barrel" — and the project, the Gravina Island Bridge at Ketchikan, Alaska. Ashdown's phrase worked.

The proposed span would have linked the city of Ketchikan by highway to the Ketchikan International Airport on Gravina Island, which was home to some fifty permanent residents. Located in the slender part of the state that sits alongside the Canadian province of British Columbia, Ketchikan is squeezed between the mountains and the sea in an area divided with fiords and valleys and cuts. Alaska is still a physically wild and rough place. Some places are only accessible by air, train, or sea.

Access to the Ketchikan airport is obtained by a ferry service that carries passengers and vehicles across the Tongass Narrows every thirty minutes. The proposed bridge would have spanned the Narrows, a commercial waterway used by both cargo and cruise ships, which would have required an extremely high and long structure. Originally proposed at a cost of $398 million, it was to be built primarily with federal funds earmarked for that purpose.[4]

Planning for the Gravina Island Bridge was well underway when Sarah took office as governor. It had been the subject of heated debate and national attention when members of Congress proposed diverting previously approved funding from the project to address rebuilding needs in New Orleans following Hurricane Katrina.

Alaska's congressional delegation had originally obtained funds earmarked for the bridge that would have left Alaska bearing only about $160 million of the costs. However, before the funding was finally appropriated, Congress removed the earmarks for that allocation. In effect, they worked money for the project into the general, undesignated grant of federal highway aid that came to the state. The project was one for which federal money could be spent, but the amount sent to Alaska did not increase from the amount normally received. If Alaska went forward with other projects for which they had been planning to use undesignated federal funds, the state's portion of the bridge project would double. In addition, cost for the project was expected to rise as the project moved from planning to actual construction.[5]

Forced to choose between the bridge and other pressing needs across the state, Governor Palin took a look at the numbers and canceled the project.[6] It wasn't an easy decision. She had campaigned in favor of the project during the election. Yet, speaking at the Republican rally in Dayton, Ohio, and later at the Republican National Convention in St. Paul, Sarah talked about the decision with bravado, saying, "I told Congress thanks but no thanks on that bridge to nowhere. If our state wanted a bridge, I said, we'd build it ourselves."[7]

What appeared to be a change of heart was not a change of policy, but rather a difficult choice dictated by the cost. The project provided a benefit, was safe, and was legally authorized, but the rise in price affected the project's priority in the governmental process. The benefit no longer outweighed the cost. As a result, the bridge project was dropped. That much Sarah Palin got right. Although many in the Alaska legislature castigated her for halting the project, Fred Dyson, a state senator from Eagle River, noted, "[She] deserves credit for trying to impose some objective criteria on the capital budget, which is essentially a huge exercise in earmarking by individual legislators."[8]

If she had been a more traditional politician, and if she had followed the lead of some previous Alaskan elected officials, Sarah might have used her inside knowledge about the project to her advantage and bought up large tracts of Gravina Island in advance of the project, built the bridge at any cost, dumped the cost on the unsuspecting citizens of Alaska, and developed the island as a home for wealthy retirees. The people of Ketchikan would have been delighted, and many in the public would have remained unaware. But that wasn't Sarah Palin.

Instead, even though her decision was an unpopular one and was also a step away from the support for the project she had implied during her campaign for office, Sarah came to it in good order: applying well-defined criteria to the proposal and analyzing the data by those criteria. The people of Ketchikan might have been disappointed in losing the project, but it was hard to argue with the logic. The difficult part was telling the people of Gravina Island that they would have to keep using the ferry. That part Sarah *did not* handle well. Announcing the cut did not fair so well.

Rather than hearing the news firsthand from the governor, the people of Ketchikan heard the news through the media.[9] Even though she had traveled to Ketchikan during the gubernatorial campaign and voiced support for the bridge, Sarah did not return to tell them she had cut the project from the budget or to explain why.

Moreover, citizens of Ketchikan listening as Sarah was introduced to the nation as John McCain's running mate, and again as she accepted the nomination at the Republican National Convention, heard her brag to the audience about how she had turned Congress down on the project. Her gleeful use of the phrase "Bridge to Nowhere," and doing so for the sake of winning the audience's favor, smacked of the old-style politics-as-usual she had spent a lifetime denouncing. As one would expect, her remarks didn't go over well in and around Ketchikan.[10]

In spite of how she has explained her remarks since then,[11] Sarah's presentation of how the project came to be halted wasn't altogether consistent with the facts.[12] She had not told Congress anything. Congress had made its own decision about how to convey federal highway funds to the State of Alaska. As governor, Sarah could have spent the money on the bridge; she just couldn't have the bridge and the other items on the state's highway priority list too.

Everyone wants to be popular, and one way to gain that acclaim is by giving people what they want. Sarah could have avoided the flap over the bridge project by simply approving it and letting other highway projects slide. That would have given her the adulation of the citizens of Ketchikan, but would have set her at odds with John McCain's stance against earmarked, pork barrel, preferential spending. Elected officials are sent to office to make good decisions, even when those decisions are tough. Sometimes the complexities of the issues governing officials face place them in a position where neither choice is pleasant. Still, someone must decide and move on. Sarah Palin has shown a genuine ability to do just that.

When Sarah was elected mayor of Wasilla, she set about making changes in the way things had always operated. Those changes included firing several city hall employees, some of whom had supported her opponent. One of the people she fired was Irl Stambaugh, the chief of police. While others went away quietly into the night, Stambaugh filed a lawsuit. Defending that suit cost the city in legal fees, time, and expense, all of which could have probably been avoided.

In Wasilla, as in most small towns in America, everyone tends to know everyone's business. No doubt, news and rumors of the decisions Sarah made spread quickly. Still, if election results are any indication of approval, the voters didn't seem to mind.

In 1992, when she first ran for city council, Sarah won handily, defeating John Hartrick, her nearest rival, by more than 200 votes.[13] When she faced re-election in 1995, she took 68 percent of the vote.[14] In 1996 she unseated John Stein, the three-term incumbent, by well over 200 votes.[15] When she ran for re-election to a second term, following the earlier controversies, she defeated Stein once more, this time 909 votes to 292.[16]

As governor, Sarah Palin garnered a 90 percent approval rating, an astounding feat in politics.[17] She didn't obtain that rating by seeking the rating. She obtained it by serving the people who elected her to office, making good decisions using objective criteria, and letting the consequences fall where they may.

Like Harry Truman, Sarah led by charting a course aided by a clear sense of right and wrong. As a member of the city council she favored a newly passed sales tax even though conventional wisdom said it would sound the death knell of the local economy. She made that decision, despite the risks involved, because she believed it was in the best interests of the town. As it turns out, she was correct.

As mayor, Sarah fired department heads and started over. She did that even though it was unpopular — so unpopular that a group of citizens and disgruntled employees began agitating for a recall vote to oust her from office.

As governor, one of Sarah's first acts was to halt several projects approved by her predecessor at the last minute, among them the Bridge to Nowhere. She made those decisions because she thought they were right, not because she wanted short-term popularity.

When Sarah saw corruption she reported it and pressured responsible government officials for an investigation, even when it meant putting her political future on the line. That was a decision she was certain was correct, even though it made her extremely unpopular with the people who appointed her to her job.

Sarah Palin didn't set out to become popular. She set out to be the best leader she could be. Popularity followed. By focusing on correct priorities and by discharging the duties of her office at each level with an eye for what was right and wrong, she attained both the right decision and, ultimately, the approval others might abandon their values to find. Those who aspire to lead others would do well to follow Sarah Palin's example.

CHAPTER 12

A NEW KIND
OF LEADER

★

While I was at it, I got rid of a few things
in the governor's office that I didn't believe
our citizens should have to pay for. That luxury jet
was over the top. I put it on eBay.

Sarah Palin

Because power corrupts, society's demands
for moral authority and character increase as
the importance of the position increases.

John Adams

THE STORY OF SARAH PALIN'S POLITICAL ASCENT COULD BE told in many ways. On the one hand, it is the story of an underdog, forced to rely on grit, determination, and heart rather than on expertise or old-boy-network political clout. On the other hand, her story is an episodic journey down the open road, traveling from one experience and opportunity to the next with all the pieces falling into place at precisely the right moment. Sarah was a mother trying to make her son's education the best it could be by volunteering at his school. Dominoes toppled from there, and where they may ultimately lead is still unknown.

The connection Sarah had with constituents—the way they appreciated her seemingly honest and forthright manner—led many of them to vote for her even though they knew she disagreed with them on critical issues. Their reaction brings to mind former President Ronald Reagan. When asked what he thought voters saw in him, Reagan replied, "Would you laugh if I told you that I think, maybe, they see themselves, and that I'm one of them?"[1] Alaska voters certainly seemed to find themselves in Sarah Palin, even as she found herself in them.

Those who consider Sarah a friend think she is the most honest, forthright, caring person they know. The best. "Our Sarah," they would say. Others who, for whatever reason, had an unpleasant experience with her think she is quite the opposite. Critics point to the disgruntled as evidence that she isn't who she claims to be. Supporters emphasize that no one is liked by everyone they meet.

At the beginning of this book I set out to explore Sarah Palin's life through the lens of ten aspects of her leadership style made evident by the events of her life. This is not an attempt to suggest that she is a perfect leader or that she is right for the office she seeks. The American people will make that decision. I only suggest that her leadership style is one that effective leaders will tend to model in this century.

Leaders of the twenty-first century will look more like Sarah Palin than like traditional political leaders of the past. They will have less depth of experience and specialized skill, and they will be more adept at making decisions and connecting with voters. They will be able to organize their efforts to focus their energy on a few key topics that matter most, while moving quickly and nimbly from issue to issue. They will be agile and adaptive. They will lead by improvisation in an environment that is constantly changing. How well they perform the duties of their office will depend more on the character of their moral center than on their command of policy details.

The difficulty with a leader whose strength lies in a willingness to decide and a penchant for connecting with voters is obvious. She will be more reliant than ever on the people around her. Complex issues often turn on subtle nuances obvious only to one who takes the time for thoughtful, considered study from a comprehensive knowledge of an issue's history and details. To succeed, a leader in this age will cultivate a staff that reflects many of the same ten qualities identified in this book and reflects a lifelong work ethic, a working knowledge covering a broad range of topics, and organizing principles arising from a strong moral core.

Using the ten principles, we have viewed Sarah Palin's life from ten different angles. Seated in a circle, we have moved around her life, stopping to view her from ten different positions. What we have seen is a person whose worldview tells her: more is less, defeat is victory, progress comes not in a straight line, and value is intrinsic. She lives in harmony with her worldview as completely as any leader on the national stage.

Since she is authentically herself, what voters see in Sarah Palin is what they get. The thing that surprises people is not their assessment of her—that assessment is rather accurate. On paper, she has been in over her head in every office she has held. Rather, what surprises people the most is the connection she has made with voters. With hand-lettered signs and a band of volunteers, she took a town and then a state by storm. It was the same in every campaign that she has entered except one, and even then—finishing second to Loren Leman in the 2002 lieutenant governor's race—she emerged in a more advantageous position than she would be in had she been elected to that office.

Chapters in her story remain unsettled and unsettling. Questions raised by "Troopergate" and the firing of Walt Monegan are troublesome. Sarah insists she has nothing to hide, but evidence revealed from the ongoing investigation gives rise to more questions. Like Whitewater, there doesn't appear to be anything substantively illegal in the alleged conduct, but the incident won't quite go away, either.

Governor Palin's explanation of her remarks about the Bridge to Nowhere appear disingenuous at best. When she says she told Congress "thanks but no thanks" on the project, she isn't quite correct. She didn't tell Congress anything. Congress told her no on the earmark, and she told Ketchikan no on the bridge. For most, the discrepancy doesn't seem to really matter and, except for residents of Ketchikan, it doesn't appear to be a substantive campaign issue. Yet the notion that she would describe that incident with a nuance that glosses over accurate facts, in an apparent effort to gain points with her constituency, leaves a hint of doubt about the authenticity and transparency of her other policy statements.

In the same way, the timing of her ethics complaint against Gregg Renkes, the state attorney general, provides just enough room to question her motives. She made that complaint while sidelined after resigning from the Murkowski administration. One could say it was an opportunistic attempt to keep her name before the people. At the very least, it suggests once more a question about the accuracy of the way in which she portrays herself as "just a hockey mom who showed up and got involved."

In the 2006 governor's race, Sarah Palin campaigned on her reputation as an ethics reformer. After the primaries she faced a well-funded Democratic opponent with an organization honed to deliver a first-class campaign. Yet, just as the fall campaign battle was about to begin, federal agents raided the offices of six state legislators, making public an undercover bribery investigation.

Ethics issues filled the news. The campaign of her Democratic opponent never got on track. One is left wondering how that campaign would have ended had the attention been focused on different issues.

Still, in every campaign the final outcome came down to Sarah. She wasn't selling her expertise or her experience, and she never tried to hide that fact. All she was promoting was her self-integrity and opinions about issues. Voters saw that as honesty, a quality not always seen in the culture of politics. For a change, a politician wasn't trying to buy their vote by selling them a program or a solution or a project. She didn't make promises about solving detailed issues; she only promised one thing: "I'll listen." To win an election, Sarah was simply selling Sarah, traveling the state, and telling voters she would listen to their issues and concerns. Her opponents had more time in public office, more business experience, and more money to spend on their campaigns. None of that mattered.

Tuckerman Babcock, a former Alaska Republican Party chairman, commenting on Sarah's 2006 gubernatorial campaign said, "It's the most remarkable campaign I've ever seen. She's just running as Sarah Palin and talking about whatever comes up."[2]

Voters sit in the same position as Sarah. Faced with a growing mountain of details about her life, voters will sort through that data, categorize it by the values they hold, and come to a conclusion about her. It isn't difficult. They have been doing this for a long time in the decisions they make every day. They have the tools to decide. All they have to do is (1) apply the principles, (2) categorize the information by the issues that arise from their moral core, (3) weigh the evidence about her on those issues that compete with each other in an objective analysis, (4) avoid making a decision based on fear, and (5) move forward. To borrow from the words of Sarah Palin herself, "It's not rocket science."[3]

Perhaps it was no accident that Sarah, a former basketball player, was introduced to the nation by John McCain at center court in a basketball arena. A state basketball championship had been a defining moment in her life—a moment that convinced her there is no limit to the height of success she can attain, save that of her willingness to work.

In that respect, Sarah's story is truly American. A story of a small town girl making good. Of obstacles met and overcome by ingenuity, resourcefulness, and a belief in the goodness of others. Of a life come full circle on a lesson learned at an early age. Whatever life may hold for her in the future, it is certain that she has raised the level of the nation's discussion about itself and has placed squarely before us the proposition that leadership of this nation is in our own hands.

GOVERNOR SARAH PALIN OF ALASKA

ADDRESS OF THE VICE PRESIDENTIAL NOMINEE

TO THE REPUBLICAN NATIONAL CONVENTION

SEPTEMBER 3, 2008

Mr. Chairman, delegates, and fellow citizens: I am honored to be considered for the nomination for Vice President of the United States....

I accept the call to help our nominee for president to serve and defend America.

I accept the challenge of a tough fight in this election ... against confident opponents ... at a crucial hour for our country.

And I accept the privilege of serving with a man who has come through much harder missions ... and met far graver challenges ... and knows how tough fights are won—the next president of the United States, John S. McCain.

It was just a year ago when all the experts in Washington counted out our nominee because he refused to hedge his commitment to the security of the country he loves.

With their usual certitude, they told us that all was lost — there was no hope for this candidate who said that he would rather lose an election than see his country lose a war.

But the pollsters and pundits overlooked just one thing when they wrote him off.

They overlooked the caliber of the man himself — the determination, resolve, and sheer guts of Senator John McCain. The voters knew better.

And maybe that's because they realize there is a time for politics and a time for leadership ... a time to campaign and a time to put our country first.

Our nominee for president is a true profile in courage, and people like that are hard to come by.

He's a man who wore the uniform of this country for twenty-two years and refused to break faith with those troops in Iraq who have now brought victory within sight.

And as the mother of one of those troops, that is exactly the kind of man I want as commander in chief. I'm just one of many moms who'll say an extra prayer each night for our sons and daughters going into harm's way.

Our son Track is nineteen. And one week from tomorrow — September 11th — he'll deploy to Iraq with the Army infantry in the service of his country.

My nephew Kasey also enlisted and serves on a carrier in the Persian Gulf.

My family is proud of both of them and of all the fine men and women serving the country in uniform. Track is the eldest of our five children.

In our family, it's two boys and three girls in between — my strong and kind-hearted daughters Bristol, Willow, and Piper.

And in April, my husband Todd and I welcomed our littlest one into the world, a perfectly beautiful baby boy named Trig. From the inside, no family ever seems typical. That's how it is with us. Our family has the same ups and downs as any other ... the same challenges and the same joys.

Sometimes even the greatest joys bring challenge. And children with special needs inspire a special love. To the families of special-needs children all across this country, I have a message:

For years, you sought to make America a more welcoming place for your sons and daughters. I pledge to you that if we are elected, you will have a friend and advocate in the White House.

Todd is a story all by himself. He's a lifelong commercial fisherman ... a production operator in the oil fields of Alaska's North Slope ... a proud member of the United Steel Workers Union ... and world champion snow machine racer.

Throw in his Yup'ik Eskimo ancestry, and it all makes for quite a package.

We met in high school, and two decades and five children later, he's still my guy.

My Mom and Dad both worked at the elementary school in our small town. And among the many things I owe them is one simple lesson: that this is America, and every woman can walk through every door of opportunity.

My parents are here tonight, and I am so proud to be the daughter of Chuck and Sally Heath.

Long ago, a young farmer and haberdasher from Missouri followed an unlikely path to the vice presidency. A writer observed: "We grow good people in our small towns, with honesty, sincerity, and dignity."

I know just the kind of people that writer had in mind when he praised Harry Truman. I grew up with those people. They are the ones who do some of the hardest work in America ... who grow our food, run our factories, and fight our wars. They love their country, in good times and bad, and they're always proud of America.

I had the privilege of living most of my life in a small town. I was just your average hockey mom, and signed up for the PTA because I wanted to make my kids' public education better.

When I ran for city council, I didn't need focus

groups and voter profiles because I knew those voters, and knew their families too.

Before I became governor of the great State of Alaska, I was mayor of my hometown.

And since our opponents in this presidential election seem to look down on that experience, let me explain to them what the job involves.

I guess a small-town mayor is sort of like a "community organizer," except that you have actual responsibilities. I might add that in small towns, we don't quite know what to make of a candidate who lavishes praise on working people when they are listening, and then talks about how bitterly they cling to their religion and guns when those people aren't listening. We tend to prefer candidates who don't talk about us one way in Scranton and another way in San Francisco.

As for my running mate, you can be certain that wherever he goes, and whoever is listening, John McCain is the same man.

I'm not a member of the permanent political establishment. And I've learned quickly, these past few days, that if you're not a member in good standing of the Washington elite, then some in the media consider a candidate unqualified for that reason alone.

But here's a little news flash for all those reporters and commentators: I'm not going to Washington to seek their good opinion—I'm going to Washington to serve the people of this country. Americans expect us to go to Washington for the right reasons, and not just to mingle with the right people.

Politics isn't just a game of clashing parties and competing interests. The right reason is to challenge the status quo, to serve the common good, and to leave this nation better than we found it.

No one expects us to agree on everything. But we are expected to govern with integrity, good will, clear convictions, and ... a servant's heart.

I pledge to all Americans that I will carry myself in this spirit as vice president of the United States. This was the spirit that brought me to the governor's office, when I took on the old politics as usual in Juneau, when I stood up to the special interests, the lobbyists, big oil companies, and the good-ol' boys network.

Sudden and relentless reform never sits well with entrenched interests and power brokers. That's why true reform is so hard to achieve. But with the support of the citizens of Alaska, we shook things up. And in short order we put the government of our state back on the side of the people.

I came to office promising major ethics reform, to end the culture of self-dealing. And today, that ethics reform is the law.

While I was at it, I got rid of a few things in the

governor's office that I didn't believe our citizens should have to pay for.

That luxury jet was over the top. I put it on eBay. I also drive myself to work.

And I thought we could muddle through without the governor's personal chef—although I've got to admit that sometimes my kids sure miss her. I came to office promising to control spending—by request if possible and by veto if necessary.

Senator McCain also promises to use the power of veto in defense of the public interest—and as a chief executive, I can assure you it works. Our state budget is under control. We have a surplus.

And I have protected the taxpayers by vetoing wasteful spending: nearly half a billion dollars in vetoes.

I suspended the state fuel tax and championed reform to end the abuses of earmark spending by Congress.

I told the Congress "thanks, but no thanks," for that Bridge to Nowhere. If our state wanted a bridge, we'd build it ourselves.

When oil and gas prices went up dramatically and filled up the state treasury, I sent a large share of that revenue back where it belonged—directly to the people of Alaska.

And despite fierce opposition from oil company lobbyists, who kind of liked things the way they were, we broke their monopoly on power and resources.

As governor, I insisted on competition and basic fairness to end their control of our state and return it to the people.

I fought to bring about the largest private-sector infrastructure project in North American history. And when that deal was struck, we began a nearly forty-billion-dollar natural gas pipeline to help lead America to energy independence. That pipeline, when the last section is laid and its valves are opened, will lead America one step farther away from dependence on dangerous foreign powers that do not have our interests at heart.

The stakes for our nation could not be higher. When a hurricane strikes in the Gulf of Mexico, this country should not be so dependent on imported oil that we are forced to draw from our Strategic Petroleum Reserve. And families cannot throw away more and more of their paychecks on gas and heating oil.

With Russia wanting to control a vital pipeline in the Caucasus, and to divide and intimidate our European allies by using energy as a weapon, we cannot leave ourselves at the mercy of foreign suppliers.

To confront the threat that Iran might seek to cut off nearly a fifth of world energy supplies ... or that terrorists might strike again at the Abqaiq facility in Saudi Arabia ... or that Venezuela might shut off its oil deliveries ... we Americans need to produce more of our own oil and gas.

And take it from a gal who knows the North Slope of Alaska: we've got lots of both.

Our opponents say, again and again, that drilling will not solve all of America's energy problems—as if we all didn't know that already. But the fact that drilling won't solve every problem is no excuse to do nothing at all.

Starting in January, in a McCain-Palin administration, we're going to lay more pipelines ... build more nuclear plants ... create jobs with clean coal ... and move forward on solar, wind, geothermal, and other alternative sources.

We need American energy resources, brought to you by American ingenuity and produced by American workers.

I've noticed a pattern with our opponent. Maybe you have, too. We've all heard his dramatic speeches before devoted followers. And there is much to like and admire about our opponent. But listening to him speak, it's easy to forget that this is a man who has authored two memoirs but not a single major law or reform—not even in the state senate.

This is a man who can give an entire speech about the wars America is fighting and never use the word "victory" except when he's talking about his own campaign. But when the cloud of rhetoric has passed ... when the roar of the crowd fades away ... when the stadium lights go out, and those Styrofoam Greek columns are hauled back to some studio lot—what exactly is our opponent's plan? What does he actually seek to accomplish, after he's done turning back the waters and healing the planet? The answer is to make government bigger ... take more of your money ... give you more orders from Washington ... and to reduce the strength of America in a dangerous world. America needs more energy ... our opponent is against producing it.

Victory in Iraq is finally in sight ... he wants to forfeit.

Terrorist states are seeking nuclear weapons without delay ... he wants to meet them without preconditions.

Al-Qaeda terrorists still plot to inflict catastrophic harm on America ... he's worried that someone won't read them their rights? Government is too big ... he wants to grow it. Congress spends too much ... he promises more. Taxes are too high ... he wants to raise them. His tax increases are the fine print in his economic plan, and let me be specific.

The Democratic nominee for president supports plans to raise income taxes ... raise payroll taxes ... raise investment income taxes ... raise the death tax ... raise business taxes ... and increase the tax burden on the American people by hundreds of billions of dollars.

My sister Heather and her husband have just built a service station that's now opened for business—like millions of others who run small businesses. How are they going to be any better off if taxes go up? Or maybe you're trying to keep your job at a plant in Michigan or Ohio ... or create jobs with clean coal from Pennsylvania or West Virginia ... or keep a small farm in the family right here in Minnesota.

How are you going to be better off if our opponent adds a massive tax burden to the American economy? Here's how I look at the choice Americans face in this election.

In politics, there are some candidates who use change to promote their careers. And then there are those, like John McCain, who use their careers to promote change. They're the ones whose names appear on laws and landmark reforms, not just on buttons and banners, or on self-designed presidential seals.

Among politicians, there is the idealism of high-flown speechmaking, in which crowds are stirringly summoned to support great things. And then there is the idealism of those leaders, like John McCain, who actually do great things. They're the ones who are good for more than talk ... the ones we have always been able to count on to serve and defend America. Senator McCain's record of actual achievement and reform helps explain why so many special interests, lobbyists, and comfortable committee chairmen in Congress have fought the prospect of a McCain presidency—from the primary election of 2000 to this very day.

Our nominee doesn't run with the Washington herd. He's a man who's there to serve his country, and not just his party. A leader who's not looking for a fight, but is not afraid of one either.

Harry Reid, the Majority Leader of the current do-nothing Senate, not long ago summed up his feelings about our nominee. He said, quote, "I can't stand John McCain."

Ladies and gentlemen, perhaps no accolade we hear this week is better proof that we've chosen the right man. Clearly what the Majority Leader was driving at is that he can't stand up to John McCain. That is only one more reason to take the maverick of the Senate and put him in the White House.

My fellow citizens, the American presidency is not supposed to be a journey of "personal discovery." This world of threats and dangers is not just a community, and it doesn't just need an organizer.

And though both Senator Obama and Senator Biden have been going on lately about how they are always, quote, "fighting for you," let us face the matter squarely.

There is only one man in this election who has ever really fought for you ... in places where winning means survival and defeat means death ... and that man is

John McCain. In our day, politicians have readily shared much lesser tales of adversity than the nightmare world in which this man, and others equally brave, served and suffered for their country.

It's a long way from the fear and pain and squalor of a six-by-four cell in Hanoi to the Oval Office. But if Senator McCain is elected president, that is the journey he will have made. It's the journey of an upright and honorable man — the kind of fellow whose name you will find on war memorials in small towns across this country, only he was among those who came home.

To the most powerful office on earth, he would bring the compassion that comes from having once been powerless ... the wisdom that comes even to the captives, by the grace of God ... the special confidence of those who have seen evil, and seen how evil is overcome.

A fellow prisoner of war, a man named Tom Moe of Lancaster, Ohio, recalls looking through a pin-hole in his cell door as Lieutenant Commander John McCain was led down the hallway, by the guards, day after day. As the story is told, "When McCain shuffled back from torturous interrogations, he would turn toward Moe's door and flash a grin and thumbs up" — as if to say, "We're going to pull through this." My fellow Americans, that is the kind of man America needs to see us through these next four years.

For a season, a gifted speaker can inspire with his words.

For a lifetime, John McCain has inspired with his deeds.

If character is the measure in this election ... and hope the theme ... and change the goal we share, then I ask you to join our cause. Join our cause and help America elect a great man as the next president of the United States.

Thank you all, and may God bless America.

"Remarks as Prepared for Delivery by Alaska Governor Sarah Palin," at the 2008 Republican National Convention, St. Paul; http://portal.gop convention2008.com/speech/details.aspx?id=38.

MAJOR EVENTS
IN THE LIFE
OF SARAH PALIN

★

1964   Is born as Sarah Louise Heath in Sandpoint,
Idaho

       Moves to Skagway, Alaska

1969   Moves to Anchorage

1971   Moves to Wasilla

1976   Is baptized at a summer Bible camp

1982   Is member of high school state championship
basketball team

       Graduates from Wasilla High School

1984   Is crowned Miss Wasilla in beauty pageant

1987	Graduates from the University of Idaho
1988	Marries Todd Palin
1989	Gives birth to son Track
1990	Gives birth to daughter Bristol
1992	Is elected to Wasilla City Council
1994	Gives birth to daughter Willow
1996	Is elected mayor of Wasilla
2001	Gives birth to daughter Piper Indy
2003–4	Serves as member of the Alaska Oil and Gas Conservation Commission
2004	Makes unsuccessful run for lieutenant governor nomination
2006	Is elected governor of the State of Alaska
2008	Gives birth to son Trig
	Is Republican Party nominee for vice president

SOURCES

Chapter 1: From Wasilla to Washington

1. Transcript of John McCain's remarks introducing Sarah Palin as his running mate, taken from "McCain and Palin in Dayton, Ohio," *The New York Times*, August 29, 2008. See also, "The Hot Sun, the Signs and Wright State," posted on Kentnewsnet.com, a partnership of independent news media at Kent State University, August 29, 2008.

2. Ibid.

3. See generally, video of John McCain introducing Sarah Palin as his running mate August 29, 2008, as broadcast by CNN Network, Atlanta, viewed online at www.cnn.com. See also, amateur handheld video shot by two men in the stands at that event, viewed on Google Video.

Chapter 2: Weakness Is the New Strength

1. Kaylene Johnson, *Sarah: How a Hockey Mom Turned Alaska's Political Establishment Upside Down* (Kenmore, WA: Epicenter Press, 2008), 68.

2. Ibid., 68. "In those days, before all the scandals, we thought the sun rose and set on Stevens and Murkowski," [Judy] Patrick said (brackets mine).

3. Interview with Loren Leman, September 7, 2008.

4. See generally, "Palin Explains Her Actions in Ruedrich Case," *Anchorage Daily News*, originally published September 19, 2004, reposted online August 29, 2008, at www.adn.com.

5. Interview with Gloria Shriver Ruedrich, September 8, 2008.

6. "Palin Explains Her Actions in Ruedrich Case."

7. Johnson, *Sarah: How a Hockey Mom Turned Alaska's Political Establishment Upside Down*, 89.

8. Taken from the blog of a classmate identified only by his site name, Gun Toting Liberal, who insisted on anonymity for other reasons, www.guntotingliberal.com. Confirmed by e-mail, September 11, 2008.

9. "Meet Alaska's Hunting, Snowmobiling Governor," KITV, Honolulu, August 29, 2008, retrieved from www.kitv.com.

10. Interview with Governor Palin, behind the scenes video, Greta Van Sustren, "On the Record," Fox News Channel, aired week of September 7, 2008.

11. "Palin Seeks Republican Nomination for Governor," Associated Press, *Juneau Empire*, October 2005, retrieved August 29, 2008, from www.juneauempire.com.

12. "Palin and Experience," *Anchorage Daily News*, article previously published in print, reposted online September 2, 2008, at www.adn.com. Also, "Novice Stands Her Ground on Veterans'

Turf in Alaska, *The New York Times*, October 29, 2006; "Part 2: Rebel Status Has Fueled Front-Runner's Success," *Anchorage Daily News*, October 24, 2006; "Same-sex Unions, Drugs Get Little Play," *Anchorage Daily News*, August 6, 2006.

13. See Moe Grzelakowski, *Mother Leads Best* (Chicago: Dearborn Trade Publishing, 2005).

14. Preamble, The Constitution of the United States of America.

15. Interview with the Honorable Diane Keller, Mayor of Wasilla, Alaska, September 11, 2008.

Chapter 3: Sacrifice Ambition to Get Ahead

1. "Todd Palin," Wikipedia, retrieved from www.wikipedia.org, August 29, 2008.

2. "Palin's Parents Live a Life of Affinity with Wilderness," *Juneau Empire*, November 25, 2007. See generally, Kaylene Johnson, *Sarah: How a Hockey Mom Turned Alaska's Political Establishment Upside Down* (Kenmore, WA: Epicenter Press, 2008), 15–23. Also, "Sarah Palin," Wikipedia, retrieved from www.wikipedia.org, August 29, 2008.

3. "Palin's Parents Surprised by VP Nomination," Associated Press, *Fort Worth Star-Telegram*, August 29, 2008. Also, "Sarah Smile," *Alaska Dispatch*, August 2006, reposted online August 29, 2008.

4. "Mayor Palin: A Rough Record," *The New York Times*, September 2, 2008.

5. Ibid.

6. Johnson, *Sarah: How a Hockey Mom Turned Alaska's Political Establishment Upside Down*, 40–44.

7. Ibid.

8. Ibid., 43. See also, "'Fresh Face' Launched Palin," *Anchorage Daily News*, October 23, 2006.

9. Interview with the Honorable Diane Keller, Mayor of Wasilla, Alaska, September 11, 2008.

10. Attachment "A," City of Wasilla, Regular Election, October 6, 1992.

11. "'Fresh Face' Launched Palin," *Anchorage Daily News*, October 23, 2006.

12. Attachment "A," City of Wasilla, Regular Election, October 3, 1995.

13. Johnson, *Sarah: How a Hockey Mom Turned Alaska's Political Establishment Upside Down*, 43.

14. Attachment "A," City of Wasilla, Regular Election, October 1, 1996.

15. "The Murkowski Administration Achievements," the online archives, www.frankmurkowski.com. See also, Citizens for Ethical Government: "Frank H. Murkowski: Campaign Finance /Money — Summary — Senator 2002," at http://citizens4 ethics.com/category/cfeg/home/background-documents/ frank-murkowski/. See also, "Frank Murkowski," Wikipedia, retrieved from www.wikipedia.org.

16. See generally, Johnson, *Sarah: How a Hockey Mom Turned Alaska's Political Establishment Upside Down*, 67–72.

17. Interview with Loren Leman, September 7, 2008. See also, "Wasilla Mayor Shines at Forum," *Fairbanks Daily News-Miner*, August 7, 2002.

18. "'Fresh Face' Launched Palin."

19. "Part 2: Rebel Status Has Fueled Front-Runner's Success," *Anchorage Daily News*, October 24, 2006.

Chapter 4: True North Never Changes

1. "Palin Has Not Pushed Creation Science as Alaska Governor," *Fairbanks Daily News-Miner*, September 3, 2008.
2. Kaylene Johnson, *Sarah: How a Hockey Mom Turned Alaska's Political Establishment Upside Down* (Kenmore, WA: Epicenter Press, 2008), 24–27.
3. "Baptized at Little Beaver Lake Camp," from Sarah Palin's remarks to the Master's Commission class at Wasilla Assembly of God, viewed at www.youtube.com.
4. Johnson, *Sarah: How a Hockey Mom Turned Alaska's Political Establishment Upside Down*, 26.
5. "Brief History of the Assemblies of God," obtained from the denominational website at www.ag.org.
6. See "Statement of Fundamental Truths," available online at www.ag.org and in a condensed version in *Our 16 Doctrines*, a pamphlet published by Gospel Publishing House, Springfield, Missouri, 2005.
7. "Sarah Palin Profile: Former Beauty Queen Was an Unlikely Choice," www.Telegraph.co.uk, September 1, 2008. Also, "How Religion Guides Palin," *Chicago Tribune*, September 6, 2008.
8. Interview with the Reverend David Pepper, pastor of Church on the Rock, Wasilla, Alaska, September 10, 2008.
9. "Bible Is Palin's Professional Guide, Friends and Pastors Say," *International Herald Tribune*, September 7, 2008.
10. For a survey discussion of moral development, see "Moral Development and Moral Education: An Overview," University of Illinois at Chicago, found online at http://tigger.uic.edu/~Inucci/MoralEd/overview.html.
11. See generally, "Ronald Wilson Reagan," *Washington Post*, June 6, 2004.
12. "Bible Is Palin's Profession Guide, Friends and Pastor Say."

13. "Meet Alaska's Hunting, Snowmobiling Governor," KITV, Honolulu, August 29, 2008, retrieved from www.kitv.com. Also, "Arctic National Wildlife Refuge," Wikipedia, retrieved from www.wikipedia.org.; "Arctic Refuge Drilling Controversy," Wikipedia, retrieved from www.wikipedia.org.

14. Johnson, *Sarah: How a Hockey Mom Turned Alaska's Political Establishment Upside Down*, 36–38.

15. Ibid., 37–38.

16. "Bible Is Palin's Professional Guide, Friends and Pastors Say." In that article, Janet Kincaid, who served on some Wasilla boards and commissions while Sarah was mayor, commented on the consistent theme of Sarah's spiritual path and says, "The churches that Sarah has attended all believe in a literal translation of the Bible. Her principal ethical and moral beliefs stem from this."

17. Constitution of the State of Alaska, Article VIII, retrieved online from www.alaska.gov.

18. The Honorable Sarah Palin, Governor of Alaska, 2008 State of the State Address, January 15, 2008.

19. "An Apostle of Alaska," *Newsweek*, September 15, 2008.

20. Ibid.

21. "Part 2: Rebel Status Has Fueled Front-Runner's Success," *Anchorage Daily News*, October 24, 2006.

22. Ibid.

23. "Father: Palin Showed Grit at Early Age," CNN Network, Atlanta, September 11, 2008, retrieved from www.cnn.com.

24. Sarah Palin, nomination speech at the Republican National Convention, St. Paul, September 3, 2008.

25. "Palin Is Ready for Return to the Public Arena and Service," *Anchorage Daily News*, previously published, reposted online at www.adn.com, September 2, 2008.

Chapter 5: Made in the USA

1. See generally, any good encyclopedia. I consulted the entry in *Merriam-Webster's Collegiate Encyclopedia* (Springfield, MA: Merriam-Webster, 2000).

2. Kaylene Johnson, *Sarah: How a Hockey Mom Turned Alaska's Political Establishment Upside Down* (Kenmore, WA: Epicenter Press, 2008), 95.

3. My assessment of the 2006 gubernatorial election. For a general sense of how the election was won, see Johnson, *Sarah: How a Hockey Mom Turned Alaska's Political Establishment Upside Down*, 93–108.

4. The Constitution of the State of Alaska, 1956 (as amended), Article 1, Section 25. Retrieved online from www.ltgov.state.ak.us.

5. Interview with Loren Leman, September 7, 2008. Also, "Same-Sex Unions, Drugs Get Little Play," *Anchorage Daily News*, August 6, 2006.

6. "Same-Sex Unions, Drugs, Get Little Play."

7. "Same-Sex Benefits Ban Gets Palin Veto," *Anchorage Daily News*, December 29, 2006. Also, interview with Loren Leman, September 7, 2008. Also, "Same-Sex Unions, Drugs Get Little Play."

8. Interview with Loren Leman, September 7, 2008.

9. "Same-Sex Benefits Ban Gets Palin Veto."

10. Ibid. Also, interview with Loren Leman, September 7, 2008.

11. "Same-Sex Benefits Ban Gets Palin Veto."

12. "Same-Sex Unions, Drugs Get Little Play."

13. "Same-Sex Benefits Ban Gets Palin Veto."

14. "Subpoenas Expected in Monegan Firing Case," *Anchorage Daily News*, September 6, 2008.

15. "Palin Denies Accusation over Firing of Monegan," *Anchorage Daily News*, July 18, 2008. Also, "Subpoenas Expected in Monegan Firing Case."

16. See "Why Walt Monegan Got Fired: Palin's Abuse of Power," "Vetting, Wooten and Troopergate," "The Real Question," and "Grading Palin's Speech," among others, posted at www.andrewhalcro.com.

17. "Kerry's Top Ten Flip-Flops," CBS News, September 29, 2004, retrieved from www.cbsnews.com.

18. "Bush's Top Ten Flip-Flops," CBS News, September 28, 2004, retrieved from www.cbsnews.com.

19. "Palin Seeks Republican Nomination for Governor," Associated Press, *Juneau Empire*, October 2005, retrieved August 29, 2008, from www.juneauempire.com.

20. Sarah Palin, acceptance speech at the Republican National Convention, St. Paul, September 3, 2008.

Chapter 6: Change Constantly

1. "Palin's Small Alaska Town Secured Big Federal Funds," *Washington Post*, September 2, 2008.

2. Interview with the Honorable Diane Keller, Mayor of Wasilla, Alaska, September 11, 2008. Mayor Keller was a member of the city council at the time of these decisions. See also, City of Wasilla, Alaska, Schedule of Expenditures of Federal Awards, 1999, 2000, 2001, and 2002. And see also, City of Wasilla, Alaska, General Governmental Revenues by Source, Last Ten Fiscal Years, included in the city's 1998 financial statement.

3. "Fact Check: Palin and The Bridge to Nowhere," Associated Press, *Washington Post*, September 8, 2006.

4. Interview with the Honorable Diane Keller, September 11, 2008.

5. "FBI Raids Legislative Offices," *Anchorage Daily News*, September 1, 2006. Also, "FBI Raids Offices of 6 Alaska Legislators," Associated Press, *Washington Post*, September 2, 2006.

6. "Bribery Charges Against Alaska Lawmakers," Associated Press, *The New York Times*, May 5, 2007.

7. See "All-Alaska Pipeline Pitch to Get 2nd Look," *Juneau Empire*, February 22, 2008. Also, "Former Governor Endorses All-Alaska Gas Pipeline," Alaska Gas Pipeline Blog, http://alaska-gas-pipeline.blogspot.com, May 25, 2008. Also, "All-Alaska Line Remains in Gas Line Debate, Despite Questions," *Fairbanks Daily News-Miner*, July 26, 2008.

8. "AGIA Passes, Palin Thanks Legislators," Governor's Press Release 08–131, August 1, 2008, found online at www.gov.state.ak.us.

9. "All Three Candidates Support Gas Line Lawsuit," *Anchorage Daily News*, November 3, 2006.

10. "AGIA Passes, Palin Thanks Legislators." (Approval of AGIA agreement with company selected under AGIA terms and standards.)

11. "Governor Battles Oil Industry, Wins Approval of AGIA," *Juneau Empire*, posted online at AlaskaLegislature.com, May 18, 2007. (Approval by legislature of enacting AGIA legislation.)

Chapter 7: Fear Is a Four-Letter Word

1. "Sarah Palin Had Turbulent First Year as Mayor of Alaska Town," *Seattle Times*, September 7, 2008.

2. "Palin's Start in Alaska: Not Politics as Usual," *The New York Times*, September 2, 2008. Also, "New Mayor, Sharp Knife," *Anchorage Daily News*, October 3, 1996.

3. "Palin's Start in Alaska: Not Politics as Usual."

4. Ibid.

5. Ibid.

6. "New Mayor, Sharp Knife."

7. "'Fresh Face' Launched Palin," *Anchorage Daily News*, October 23, 2006.

8. Ibid.

9. Ibid.

10. See City of Wasilla Municipal Code 2.16.020.

11. "Sarah Palin Had Turbulent First Year as Mayor of Alaska Town."

12. "'Fresh Face' Launched Palin."

13. "Palin's Start in Alaska: Not Politics as Usual." Also, "Sarah Palin Had Turbulent First Year as Mayor of Alaska Town."

14. "Sarah Palin Had Turbulent First Year as Mayor of Alaska Town."

15. Ibid.

16. Ibid. See also, Kaylene Johnson, *Sarah: How a Hockey Mom Turned Alaska's Political Establishment Upside Down* (Kenmore, WA: Epicenter Press, 2008), 44.

17. "'Fresh Face' Launched Palin."

18. "Sarah Palin Had Turbulent First Year as Mayor of Alaska Town."

19. See "Palin's Start in Alaska: Not Politics as Usual." See also, Johnson, *Sarah: How a Hockey Mom Turned Alaska's Political Establishment Upside Down*, 42–66.

20. "Palin's Start in Alaska: Not Politics as Usual."

21. "Attorney General's Involvement in Taiwan Coal Deal Goes Deep," Associated Press, posted at http://AlaskaLegislature. com, December 7, 2004. Also, "Scrutiny Began in September," *Anchorage Daily News*, February 6, 2005.

22. "Scrutiny Began in September." Also, "Alaska Attorney Gen-

eral Gregg Renkes to Resign," *USA Today*, February 6, 2005. Also, "Attorney General's Involvement in Taiwan Coal Deal Goes Deep."

23. Interview with Loren Leman, September 7, 2008.

24. "Alaska Attorney General Gregg Renkes to Resign." Also, interview with Loren Leman, September 7, 2008.

25. "Scrutiny Began in September."

26. See generally, Johnson, *Sarah: How a Hockey Mom Turned Alaska's Political Establishment Upside Down*, 83.

27. "Part 2: Rebel Status Has Fueled Front-Runner's Success," *Anchorage Daily News*, October 24, 2006.

Chapter 8: Work Is a Lifestyle

1. "Father: Palin Showed Grit at Early Age," CNN Network, Atlanta, September 11, 2008, www.cnn.com.

2. Kaylene Johnson, *Sarah: How a Hockey Mom Turned Alaska's Political Establishment Upside Down* (Kenmore, WA: Epicenter Press, 2008), 29–31.

3. Ibid.

4. Johnson, *Sarah: How a Hockey Mom Turned Alaska's Political Establishment Upside Down*, 29–31.

5. "Sarah Barracuda's 1982 State Championship," *Inside Edition*, September 4, 2008, retrieved online from www.insideedition. com. See also, Johnson, *Sarah: How a Hockey Mom Turned Alaska's Political Establishment Upside Down*, 29–31.

6. "Sarah Barracuda's 1982 State Championship." See also, Johnson, *Sarah: How a Hockey Mom Turned Alaska's Political Establishment Upside Down*, 29–31.

7. From Chris Boese's Weblog at www.serendipit-e.com, entered November 2006, retrieved August 29, 2008.

8. "From Sandpoint to a Shot at History," *Sandpoint Spokesman Review*, August 30, 2008.

9. "Sarah Barracuda's 1982 State Championship." See also, Johnson, *Sarah: How a Hockey Mom Turned Alaska's Political Establishment Upside Down*, 29–31.

10. "Sarah Barracuda's 1982 State Championship."

11. General information obtained from Wikipedia, at www.wikipedia.org. See also the official Robert Service High School website at www2.asd.k12.ak.us/new3/default.htm.

12. "Sarah Barracuda's 1982 State Championship." See also, Johnson, *Sarah: How a Hockey Mom Turned Alaska's Political Establishment Upside Down*, 29–31.

13. Ibid.

14. Ibid.

15. Ibid.

16. Ibid.

17. Ibid.

18. Ibid.

19. Ibid.

20. Ibid.

21. Ibid.

22. Ibid.

23. "Sarah Barracuda's 1982 State Championship."

24. "Sarah Barracuda's 1982 State Championship." See also, Johnson, *Sarah: How a Hockey Mom Turned Alaska's Political Establishment Upside Down*, 29–31.

25. "'Fresh Face' Launched Palin," *Anchorage Daily News*, October 23, 2006.

26. "Sarah Barracuda's 1982 State Championship."

27. "Father: Palin Showed Grit at Early Age."

28. "New Mayor, Sharp Knife," *Anchorage Daily News*, October 3, 1996, reposted online at www.adn.com, August 29, 2008.

29. See generally, Johnson, *Sarah: How a Hockey Mom Turned Alaska's Political Establishment Upside Down*, 15–23.

30. Ibid.

31. "Sarah Palin NRA Life Member, Fisherman & Hunter," at http://losttarget.blogspost.com. See also, "Sarah Palin and Joe Biden: Worlds Apart," at www.nraila.org/legislation/read.aspx ?id=4156.

32. Fred Thompson, before the Republican National Convention, St. Paul, September 2, 2008.

33. See generally, Johnson, *Sarah: How a Hockey Mom Turned Alaska's Political Establishment Upside Down*, 15–23.

34. "Palin's Parents Live a Life of Affinity with Wilderness," *Juneau Empire*, November 25, 2007.

35. "Father: Palin Showed Grit at Early Age."

Chapter 9: Mean It Like You Say It

1. "Palins' Child Diagnosed with Down Syndrome," *Anchorage Daily News*, April 22, 2008. Also, "Palin Balances Official Duties, Son's Needs," Associated Press, *Anchorage Daily News*, May 6, 2008.

2. "Palin Balances Official Duties, Son's Needs."

3. Ibid.

4. "Palins' Child Diagnosed with Down Syndrome." See also, "Palin Balances Official Duties, Son's Needs."

5. "Prenatal Test Puts Down Syndrome in Hard Focus," *The New York Times*, May 9, 2007. Also, "The Best Thing about Sarah Palin," *Christianity Today*, August 30, 2008.

6. "Palins' Child Diagnosed with Down Syndrome." Also, "Palin Balances Official Duties, Son's Needs."

7. Kaylene Johnson, *Sarah: How a Hockey Mom Turned Alaska's Political Establishment Upside Down* (Kenmore, WA: Epicenter Press, 2008), 88–92.

8. Interview with Loren Leman, September 7, 2008.

9. Johnson, *Sarah: How a Hockey Mom Turned Alaska's Political Establishment Upside Down*, 88–89.

10. Ibid.

11. Ibid.

12. Ibid.

13. Ibid.

14. Ibid.

15. "Governor's Son Enlists Sept. 11," *Anchorage Daily News*, September 13, 2007, reposted online August 29, 2008, at www.adn.com.

16. Sarah Palin, acceptance speech at the Republican National Convention, St. Paul, September 3, 2008.

17. "Bristol Palin's Pregnancy Was an Open Secret Back Home," *New York Daily News*, September 2, 2008.

18. Ibid.

19. "Palin Admits Her 17-Year-Old Daughter Is Pregnant," *New York Daily News*, September 1, 2008.

Chapter 10: Mother Knows Best

1. "Palin Balances Official Duties, Son's Needs," Associated Press, *Anchorage Daily News*, May 6, 2008.

2. As Moe Grzelakowski put it, "Motherhood doesn't transform immoral or even amoral individuals into saints, but it strengthens the character of good women. It deepens them. It broadens

their view. It makes them more human" (*Mother Leads Best* [Chicago: Dearborn Trade Publishing, 2005], 166).

3. Alaskan boroughs are like counties, and Mat-Su is a short form of Matananuska-Susitna, a borough named after its two prominent rivers. See "Matanuska-Susitna Borough," Wikipedia, retrieved from www.wikipedia.org, September 17, 2008. Alaska's often-mentioned North Slope is officially a borough.

4. Kaylene Johnson, *Sarah: How a Hockey Mom Turned Alaska's Political Establishment Upside Down* (Kenmore, WA: Epicenter Press, 2008), 65.

5. Interview with the Honorable Diane Keller, Mayor of Wasilla, Alaska, September 11, 2008.

6. "Governor Battles Oil Industry, Wins Approval of AGIA," http://AlaskaLegislature.com, May 18, 2007.

7. Ibid.

8. "Openness in Gas Line Negotiations Is a Critical Mistake," *Alaska Daily News*, June 22, 2008.

9. "Palin Signs AGIA License Bill," State of Alaska, Office of Governor, Press Release No. 08 – 148, August 27, 2008.

10. Johnson, *Sarah: How a Hockey Mom Turned Alaska's Political Establishment Upside Down*, 67.

11. "John McCain and Sarah Palin on Shattering the Glass Ceiling," *People Magazine*, August 29, 2008.

Chapter 11: Leadership Isn't a Beauty Contest

1. Douglas C. Foyles, *Counting the Public In: Presidents, Public Opinion, and Foreign Policy* (New York: Columbia University Press, 1999). Accessed online at Google Books.

2. "The Unusual Challenges Palin Faced in Alaska," *The New York Times*, September 3, 2008.

3. William Safire, "Bridge to Nowhere," *New York Times Magazine*, October 8, 2006.

4. The term "earmark" is often used in disparaging ways, but "earmarked" is actually an official budgetary term used by the Office of Management and Budget (OMB). It is officially defined as "funds provided by the Congress for projects or programs where the congressional direction (in bill or report language) circumvents Executive Branch merit-based or competitive allocation processes. . . ." There's more to the definition, and it gets a little complicated with "soft earmarks" and "hard earmarks," but the meaning is rather clear. When Congress "earmarks" an appropriation, the money so "earmarked" is conveyed for a specific project. The recipient of that money is required to spend the money on the designated project or return it to the federal government. See "OMB Guidance to Agencies on Definition of Earmarks," retrieved from www.omb.gov. See also, "The Budget System and Concepts," OMB official document, retrieved from www.omb.gov.

5. Interview with Loren Leman, September 7, 2008.

6. " 'Bridge to Nowhere' Abandoned," report published in 2007 by CNN Network, Atlanta, retrieved from www.cnn.com, September 9, 2008. Also, "About-Face," *Anchorage Daily News*, originally published February 8, 2008, reposted online September 5, 2008.

7. Sarah Palin, speech after John McCain announced her as his vice presidential nominee, Dayton, Ohio, August 29, 2008.

8. " 'Bridge to Nowhere' Abandoned."

9. "Palin for 'Bridge to Nowhere' Before She Was Against It," *Boston Herald*, August 31, 2008.

10. Ibid.: "Bert Stedman, a Sitka Republican who represents Ketchikan in the state senate, told the *Ketchikan Daily News* he was proud to see Palin picked for the vice-president's role,

but disheartened by her reference to the bridge. 'In the role of governor, she should be pursuing a transportation policy that benefits the state of Alaska [rather than] pandering to the southern 48,' he said."

11. See "Excerpts: Charlie Gibson Interviews GOP Vice Presidential Candidate Sarah Palin," ABC News, New York, September 12, 2008, retrieved online at www.abcnews.go.com.

12. "Some of Palin's Remarks Stretch the Truth," *Washington Post*, September 4, 2008. Also, "Fact Check: Palin and the Bridge to Nowhere," Associated Press, *Washington Post*, September 8, 2008.

13. Attachment "A," City of Wasilla, Regular Election, October 6, 1992.

14. City of Wasilla, Regular Election, October 3, 1995.

15. Attachment "A," City of Wasilla, Regular Election, October 1, 1996.

16. City of Wasilla, Regular Election, Official Results, October 5, 1999.

17. "The Most Popular Governor," *The Weekly Standard*, July 16, 2007.

Chapter 12: A New Kind of Leader

1. "Ronald Wilson Reagan," *Washington Post*, June 6, 2004.

2. "Rebel Status Has Fueled Front-Runner's Success," *Anchorage Daily News*, October 24, 2006.

3. "'Fresh Face' Launched Palin," *Anchorage Daily News*, October 23, 2006.

INDEX

The Faith

What Christians Believe, Why They Believe It, and Why It Matters

Charles Colson and Harold Fickett

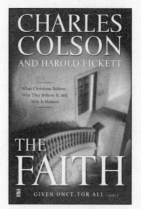

The Faith is a book for our troubled times and for decades to come. It is the most important book Chuck Colson and Harold Fickett have ever written: a thought-provoking, soul-searching, and powerful manifesto of the great, historical central truths of Christianity that have sustained believers through the centuries. Brought to immediacy with vivid, true stories, here is what Christianity is really about and why it is a religion of hope, redemption, and beauty.

Hardcover, Jacketed: 978-0-310-27603-6
Unabridged Audio CD: 978-0-310-27608-1
Audio Download,
  Unabridged: 978-0-310-27609-8

ebooks:
Adobe® Reader®
  eBook Reader®: 978-0-310-29560-0
Microsoft Reader®: 978-0-310-29564-8
Mobipocket Reader™: 978-0-310-29565-5
Palm™ Reader: 978-0-310-29566-2
Sony® Reader: 978-0-310-29567-9
ePub: 978-0-310-29563-1

Also available:

Charles Colson on Politics and the Christian

DVD: 978-0-310-28687-5

Pick up a copy today at your favorite bookstore!

ZONDERVAN®
.com

Share Your Thoughts

With the Author: Your comments will be forwarded to
the author when you send them to *zauthor@zondervan.com*.

With Zondervan: Submit your review of this book
by writing to *zreview@zondervan.com*.

Free Online Resources at
www.zondervan.com/hello

 Zondervan AuthorTracker: Be notified whenever your
favorite authors publish new books, go on tour, or post
an update about what's happening in their lives.

 Daily Bible Verses and Devotions: Enrich your life
with daily Bible verses or devotions that help you start
every morning focused on God.

 Free Email Publications: Sign up for newsletters on
fiction, Christian living, church ministry, parenting, and
more.

 Zondervan Bible Search: Find and compare
Bible passages in a variety of translations at
www.zondervanbiblesearch.com.

 Other Benefits: Register yourself to receive online
benefits like coupons and special offers, or to participate
in research.